A book for
Garrett Eversole -
Congrats on HS Graduation
Mike + Charley McGahan
June 15, 2019

"HOW CAN THEY POSSIBLY THINK LIKE THAT???"

Professional Personality Index™ Resource Guide and Self Test

Complete Test and Self Evaluation Included.

Be Sure To Take the Test on Page VII

*Dedicated to my sons Greg and Doug
whose lives are a joy to me.*

"HOW CAN THEY POSSIBLY THINK LIKE THAT???"

Professional Personality Index™ Resource Guide and Self Test

Copyright © 1992, Revised Copyright © 1998, by Lynn Ellsworth Taylor
All rights reserved

This book or any part thereof may not be reproduced by any means, written or mechanical, or be programmed into any electronic retrieval or information storage system without permission in writing from the author except in cases where short passages are used solely for the purpose of review in periodicals, television and radio. This book is intended for personal use only. Any repetitive use of the PPI test and training information by companies and individuals requires a license from the author and Elliott Bay Publishing, Inc.

First Printing April, 1992.
Library of Congress Publication Data
Taylor, Lynn Ellsworth, 1949-
1. How Can They Possibly Think Like That???
The Professional Personality Index Resource Guide

ISBN- O-9627859-54   (paper)   (Download version) $24.95

ISBN O-9627859-6-2   (Hardcover) $49.95

Manufactured in the USA by Elliott Bay Publishing, Inc.
January 1998

Foreword by: Glen Villalobos, National Executive, Human Resources, Volunteers of America.

ACKNOWLEDGMENTS

Sincere thanks and appreciation are expressed to:

Dennis Duroff for his support, encouragement and conceptual design of the graphics in this book.

Chuck Cantellay for his support in the development of book design.

Scott Rosenkranz for his final creative design of this book in its entirety.

Jerry Marble, my business partner, for his support and many years of diligent, creative work.

Glen Villalobos for his critical support and his contribution of the Foreword to this book.

About Glen Villalobos

With a Bachelor of Science degree in Business Administration from University of Redlands and a Master of Arts in Psychology and Organizational Behavior, Glen Villalobos consults with for-profit, nonprofit and community organizations.

As the developer and coordinator of the Small Business Human Resource Certification Program for the Small Business Development Center at Southeastern Louisiana University, Glen has consulted with many sizes and types of businesses. He is adjunct faculty member for Tulane University and University of New Orleans and is a certified vocational educator. He is also a certified trainer for FastTrac from the Entrepreneurial Education Foundation.

Previously, Glen was a national executive for Volunteers of America, one of the country's largest national nonprofit human service organizations, and was human resource manager for Ferranti International Signal and Hughes Aircraft Company.

Having graduated from Moderator Training School at Bethesda, Maryland based RIVA Institute, Glen is also a specialist in qualitative research and continuous quality improvement. He also served as lead facilitator for the Louisiana Economic Development Commissions, Culture, Recreation and Tourism Task Force in developing its strategic plan.

Glen is graduate of the Leadership St. Tammany West Program and currently serves as a board member and Curriculum Committee Chair. He is past president of Northshore Kiwanis and board member for the Gulf Coast International Hispanic Chamber of Commerce.

ABOUT THE TEST

What I don't know about myself controls my life.

Self knowledge is the cornerstone on which leadership is built. If I do not know and understand the ineffective ways I handle the variety of people and situations in my life. If I am not willing to change the attitudes and ideas and beliefs around which I construct these ineffective strategies. If I am not even aware of these beliefs and ideas which I keep so preciously locked away— supposedly out of sight of others— I am controlled by these things. I will find myself responding to a boss, or a peer or an employee (or spouse or child) just like I used to respond to my Father or Mother or sibling.

All of us live to some degree in this unconscious state; unaware of the stimulus and response (knee-jerk) patterns of our lives. The power of any leader derives directly from knowledge of these patterns and a willingness to become ever more conscious of them. To the degree I know myself and I am conscious of the beliefs and attitudes which control my behavior patterns; to that degree I am in control of my own life. I am awake. I am able to make choices. I can ask myself "What is the most effective response?" rather than simply reacting out of old personality scripts.

This is the power offered by the Professional Personality Index™

The test itself only takes about 3 minutes to take.
The learning lasts a life time.

Please take the test on the following two pages before you read this book.

Professional Personality Index™ Test
How to take the Professional Personality Index Test

Circle two words in each box which most relate to you-the words that have the greatest value to you. Don't spend more than 10 seconds per box.

Complete the selections from all 36 boxes on the following page. When you are done, line up the letters at the left of the page with each row of words. Count the number of times you have selected each letter (A, B, C, or D) and log these totals in the provided total area. Take these totals and plot them on the chart below. This will provide a visual reference for your...

Effective business people understand their unique approach to work and other aspects of life. This knowledge allows them to relate better to others, to be more effective and to attract others who contribute to their success. The totals from the test show which personality and leadership types you are:

A. Builder, B. Merchant,
D. Banker, C. Innovator.

These personality styles are equal in value, but have different approaches to work. All have counterbalancing weaknesses that get in the way of individual and corporate goals.

Professional Personality Index

```
    35                           35
      30                       30
        25                   25
          20               20
            15           15
              10       10
A- Builder       5   5       B- Merchant
D- Banker        5   5       C- Innovator
              10       10
            15           15
          20               20
        25                   25
      30                       30
    35                           35
```

NAME: _____

I am a: _____ _____
         DOMINANT   SECONDARY

Sample Professional Personality Index

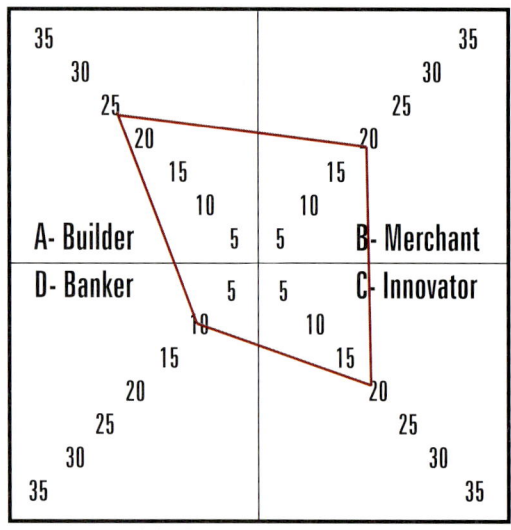

NAME John Doe
I am a: Builder   Merchant
         DOMINANT   SECONDARY

A B C D	Action Vision Strategy Planning		Reality Belief Value Proof		Smart Bright Ingenious Accurate		Quick Alert Perceptive Reliable
B C D A	Relationships Solutions Statistics Results		Excitement Evaluation Fortification Urgency		Invest Piece Together Garner/Save Buy		Opportunity Possibility Stability Focus
C D A B	Synergy Uniformity Autonomy Team Work		Balance Integrity Independence Agreement		Patience Order Drive Enthusiasm		Illustrate Expect Command Teach
D A B C	Organization Concrete Abstract Design		Information Power Motivation Systems		Resolve Effort Energy Tenacity		Advise Candor Diplomacy Process
A D B C	Authority History Unity Continuity		Initiate Document Present Configure		Activate Consolidate Stimulate Rearrange		Decisions Report Openness Appropriateness
B D C A	Diversity Detail Complexity Simplicity		Charisma Conservation Problem-solving Substance		Clever Formal Eclectic Practical		Change Maintain Consider alternatives Implement
C A B D	Pathways Bottom Line Dialogue Analysis		Direction Work Promotion Observation		Brainstorming Conflict Discussion Devil's Advocate		Puzzles Conclusions Variety Comparison
D B C A	Justice Worth Wisdom Sufficiency		Assimilation Resiliency Adroitness Efficiency		Instruct Pull Guide Push		Inform Inspire Suggest Direct
A D C B	Effective Steady Logical Courageous		Strength Precision Variety Harmony		Emotion Knowledge Intellect Heart		Righteousness Law & Order Compassion Love

© Copyright Lynn Ellsworth Taylor, November 1997

Totals: A's = ____   B's = ____   C's = ____   D's = ____

FOREWORD by Glen Villalobos
How Can They Possibly Think Like That???

One of the most challenging issues facing business owners or managers is the management of people. Effective interpersonal relations, while being extremely critical to the success of any business also can be an elusive "Holy Grail" of management

Organizations are social systems and as such are microcosms of our society. And the complexity of our society is replicated in the workplace. Attempts to offer solutions to improve interpersonal relations have been numerous, as have been the variety of approaches. Some programs teach skill fundamentals and practice certain specific behaviors to use at the correct time. Other programs seek to improve management in the workplace by using the work team concept.

One of the most consistent approaches has been to give employees a better understanding of themselves, their behavior and teach them how to relate to others with different traits or behaviors. Many assessment instruments have been developed and applied in the workplace to help employees and managers better understand themselves and the people with whom they work. These instruments have been somewhat successful. However, the principles on which these instruments are based were developed in the 1920's by psychologists who were contemporaries of Sigmund Freud.

Other elements of assessment instruments relate to the norm group used to test the validity and reliability of the instruments. Many instruments have used college students as the norm group for validation purposes. Others use more diverse populations that don't necessarily reflect the population in the workplace.

The Professional Personality Index, developed by Lynn Ellsworth Taylor is the first instrument of its kind. It was developed around behaviors and personalities present in our workforce now. The norm group consists of the thousands of business owners, managers and other professionals that have provided feedback of the usefulness and accuracy of the Professional Personality Index.

Why should we develop our employees?

In order to answer that question, we must understand a distinction between training and development. Training refers to providing a skill, teaching a specific behavior or on the job training.

Development is giving employees the support, guidance and learning opportunities to prepare them to perform at higher levels, in higher level functions and to give them the tools to: 1) determine what developmental needs they have and 2) be inspired to improve themselves.

Often, employers attribute an employee performance problem to a lack of training. For example, a supervisor or manager who is having morale problems in the work group is often sent to management training. The employer expects this training will "take" and the supervisor/manager will come back from training re-born into a great leader of people.

The reality of this situation is that there are often other factors besides a lack of supervisor/management training that may be causing the morale problem. There are many elements in the system that can have an effect such as the policies and procedures, working conditions or the work itself. Often the more critical issues are personality based communication skills, power and control issues, and the application of inappropriate and ineffective tactics such as intimidation, interrogation, manipulation and passive aggressive behavior. If these issues are present, management training is not likely to be the answer.

The best way to determine what if any kind of training should be conducted is through a needs assessment. This is a process where job standards are compared with employee performance. Not only will a needs assessment reveal whether or not a lack of training is at the source of the problem, it will also reveal what specific type of training is needed.

Taylor's Professional Personality Index effectively identifies behavioral issues and personal value structures. The first step in all training is to excite a new level of curiosity in the participants. This personality profile test is an excellent tool for this phase.

Often in the course of conducting a needs assessment or otherwise analyzing the workplace, it may be determined that there is a miss-match between the work employees are performing and their capabilities, aptitudes or desires. And when this misalignment occurs, performance outcome is usually less than optimal.

The remedy for this is to better understand employees through a developmental assessment and align their work with their capabilities, aptitudes or desires. The Professional Personality Index helps any small business owner; any manager or executive better understand how to align employees within the organization.

But why go to this much trouble? Why be concerned with and then develop employees?

Rafer Johnson, the 1962 Olympic Decathlon Gold Medal Winner for the United States said it best. "Employees should be all they can be. Because if they are, the company can be all it can be."

INTRODUCTION

Lynn Ellsworth Taylor's, "How Can They Possibly Think Like That???" is the simplest, most fundamentally sound approach to personality profiling ever created. Praised by business owners, psychologists and human resource directors as brilliant and practical, this resource guide will serve any group of persons who want to increase their effectiveness as individuals and as a team.

The test is easier to take than any other test on the market, and it can be self administered and evaluated within ten minutes, allowing this profiling system to be used in short focus business situations: New employee interviews, conflict resolution, departmental restructuring, employee evaluations for promotions, etc. Other tests require hours to take, weeks to have evaluated and years to develop a comprehension of the results.

Even the more complex and comprehensive tests, however, do not delve into the practical applications of personality knowledge gained by the tests— not even close to the depth and the insight of the Professional Personality Index system. Individuals will quickly discover and relate to their Spiritual Cornerstones, and understand how these cornerstone values dictate so much of how we each think and act— how different we are from others with different cornerstones.

The Primary Social Values help individuals readily see themselves in practical settings, identifying strengths and weaknesses. Each person is able to understand better how his or her personality strategy works, as well as the how's and why's behind our negative behaviors.

The Way We Act illustrates as no other guide has ever attempted, the idiosyncracies of each personality profile and the mechanisms which occasionally make each of us ineffective.

Finally, The Basis for Success section clearly illustrates the different strategies each personality style uses in order to achieve personal success. It is easy to see where conflicts arise between persons with strong foundations in one personality style or another. Beginning with our Spiritual Cornerstones and ending with our Strategies for Success, the committed reader will discover a wealth of new understanding for personal growth, development of better relationships and greater personal power with people.

The Professional Personality Index is on its way to become the standard for personality assessment in American business.

TABLE OF CONTENTS

1. A Brief History of Business-How the Four Personality Styles Got Their Names – 1
2. The Basic Propositions – 5
3. The Four Basic Personality Styles – 9
   - A. Builders – 13
   - B. Merchants – 19
   - C. Innovators – 25
   - D. Bankers – 31
   - E. Common Traits – 37
4. The Six Primary Personality Combinations – 41
   - A. Merchant/Builders (Builder/Merchants) – 41
   - B. Builder/Innovators (Innovator/Builders) – 42
   - C. Banker/Builders (Builder/Bankers) – 43
   - D. Merchant/Innovators (Innovator/Merchants) – 44
   - E. Merchant/Bankers (Banker/Merchants) – 46
   - F. Banker/Innovators (Innovator/Bankers) – 47
   - G. Achieving Company Balance – 48
5. Everything You Always Wanted to Know About Why You Act the Way You Do, but Were Always Too Smart to Ask – 49
6. Why We Always Hurt the Ones We Love – 53
7. How Can They Think Like That? – 55
   Our Spiritual Cornerstones – 55
   - A. Bankers- Knowledge – 57
   - B. Innovators- Wisdom – 59
   - C. Merchants- Love – 61
   - D. Builders- Power – 63
   - E. Building a business with four corners – 66
   - F. How we each build our self-esteem – 66
8. How Can I Change Who I Am? – 79
9. Now That I Know Why I Hate Working with Him, What Do I Do About It? – 85
10. Control, Caretaking and Other Terrible Habits – 91
11. Development of Personnel as a Means to Corporate Success – 93
12. Learning Styles – 95
13. Building Effective Teams – 99
14. Using the Professional Personality Index to Characterize Job Positions – 103
15. Even Companies Have an Optimum Personality Index – 105
16. Employment Decisions – 107
17. Taking and Giving the Test – 109
18. No More Excuses – 113

About the Author – 116

PROFESSIONAL PERSONALITY INDEX™
Primary Social Values

BUILDER
Action
Results

MERCHANT
Vision
Relationships

BANKER
Conservation
Information

INNOVATOR
Assessment
Solutions

© Copyright Lynn Ellsworth Taylor, November 1997

A Brief History of Business

How the Four Personality Styles Got Their Names

In ancient cultures as humanity began to move from hunting and gathering to economically based societies, four principle types of business practitioners evolved:

Builders- A sturdy, action oriented group of individuals became specialized in constructing shelters and shops, building roads, pyramids, bridges. These builders also formed the armies, led the expeditions and served as high energy workers. Builders by their actions constantly created monuments to human resourcefulness and power: Productive farmlands, new businesses, conquering armies and the resulting civilizations.

Merchants- Teams of craftsmen, traders and shop owners specialized in developing new trading relationships, opening new markets, developing crafts and arts, teaching and creating channels through which trade goods could flow. Some of these Merchants also became the story-tellers, the poets and musicians, artists. They led in developing culture and literature. Merchants opened the minds of people to new visions, new opportunities.

Innovators- Independent, indomitable individuals became innovators, who specialized in developing new mechanical and technological devices and social solutions to allow Builders, Bankers and Merchants to continue their forward progress. These Innovators developed new tools, improved systems of government, new economic systems, advanced systems of theology, philosophy and psychology. They led in developing the systems and mechanisms that hold society together.

Bankers- People who concentrated their energies in learning, and gathering knowledge became Bankers who conserved resources and applied those resources toward the projects with least risk and highest opportunity. Bankers analyzed the results of all new projects, reported ineffective efforts, affirmed the reasons for each success and recorded the history of all aspects of society. Bankers stabilized societies around their best attributes and assured the continuity of core values and disciplines. They gathered, preserved and disseminated knowledge.

These four business-related names are appropriate personality styles for the Professional Personality Index because each of the personality types is unique and diverse. Historically it was the personality style of the individuals which led them into their occupational pursuits and it is the same today. Builders build, Merchants trade, Innovators solve problems and Bankers manage resources.

It is important to remember that Builders don't just build structures, they often build companies, build new sales territories, build departments, build financial empires. Bankers don't just deal with finances, although many are still involved in this arena, but Bankers will be found in sales departments, customer service, technical service, engineering, architecture, music, religion, sciences, etc. And they are powerful resources when applied correctly in each of these areas. Each business function, as a general rule must have a little of each type of personality involved in it, in the right balance, in order to achieve excellent results.

Marco Polo appears in history as a Merchant. He was excited about the opportunity of finding riches and important trade items in the far east. He set out to do just that, establishing new trade relations, outposts for supplies and roadways for access to the products of China.

He fulfilled his mission by discovering the spices of the east, creating relationships with his trading partners and bringing home new treasures, which he sold to fund his next venture. This is the nature and spirit of a Merchant, whether involved in sales, marketing, finance, agriculture, medicine, or science. Marco Polo also must have also had the builder spirit in him because he was not satisfied by having the dream. He made the journey himself and built his trade organization.

When Gutenberg developed the printing press, he was overcoming a seemingly insurmountable obstacle, the development of a means for communication to distant masses and future generations. His press opened the doors of education and political evolution. He was an innovator of the first order and the personality profile of Innovator for the Professional Personality Index was chosen as a recognition of the contributions, and the innovations of people like him.

Margaret Mead may have been a banker, concerned with knowledge, determined to uncover new facts and to log these discoveries for posterity. Her passion for detailed observation appears to have been a cornerstone of her life. The Builder in her got things done, created action and sometimes turned people away. The results of her life make a solid illustration of a Banker who invested her life well, founded in knowledge, committed to the expansion and preservation of knowledge.

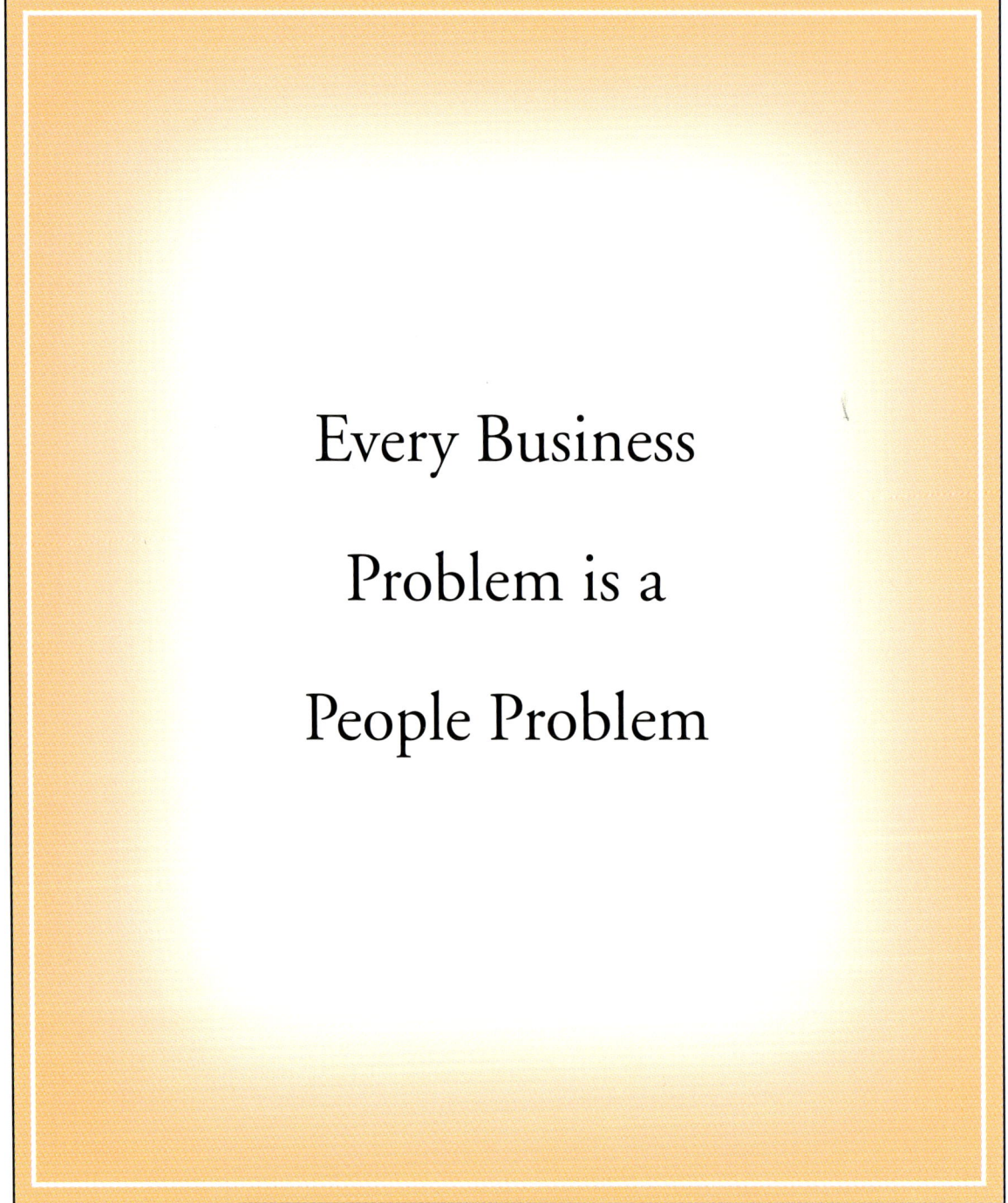

© Copyright Lynn Ellsworth Taylor, November 1997

2

The Basic Propositions

All business problems are people problems. All solutions to business challenges are people-based solutions. Is insufficient cash flow, a financial problem? Yes. But is insufficient cash flow caused by a lack of planning? Yes. Poor sales training? Yes. Over-active purchasing department? greed? fear of failure? fear of success? Yes. Yes. Yes. Yes. Cash flow problems are not simply financial problems they are leadership problems, organizational problems, ego problems— people problems.

Time after time in my work as a management consultant, I am told by a prospective client: "All I need is $500,000 to get me through this time- or, When I get the next big exciting contract I'll... or, If I could just find a bank that wasn't so stuck back in the fifties..." Every time I hear this kind of "If only" presentation, I know I am sitting across from a likely client.

Why? Because a large part of my job is helping business owners and their teams understand the truth about their situations. I have to instill accountability for the business success or failure in each member of the team and help each participant understand what his or her role is, what that role should be in order to succeed together as a team.

An equally telling list of rationalizations comes out like this: "I can't seem to get *these* people to realize... or I'm putting in eighteen hour days, *but*... or We're like one big *family* here." A lack of boundaries, rude behavior or caretaking, friction in the ranks, de-motivated leaders and followers. It's amazing how much energy is bottled up behind these flimsy excuses for mediocre performance.

These examples and many more are why I begin almost every client relationship with the development of a Professional Personality Index for each member of the company or department I am hired to improve. In addition to the opening proposition— "Every business problem is a people problem," consider the following axioms:

What I don't know about myself controls my life. It is the habits, thoughts, ideas, beliefs, fears... that I have not faced, that I am not aware of in my own life which dictate my actions and my responses. Why? Because I can only make choices about things I am conscious of. If I am not aware of a specific fear, I cannot decide to master it. If I am not conscious of a negative attitude that is limiting my performance, I am not able to decide to think differently. If I don't learn to think and believe differently I will not act differently and I will never get different results.

What I don't know about myself limits my ability to build a team around me, and frustrates me in my desire to move forward. In order to create success and to find fulfillment in my work I have to continuously increase my understanding of my basic nature and my knowledge of the personality patterns I have decided to use as strategies to get the things I want.

What I don't know about the people around me dictates the success of my business team. I may be reasonably self-aware, but without a reasonable knowledge and understanding of the people around me in the work place, communications will falter, goals and objectives will be replaced by battles for control and subterfuge. If I can't learn to change my personal strategies to fit the situation and the people involved, I am limited in the kinds of situations in which I can succeed, and in the kinds of people with whom I can succeed.

These three basic propositions must be understood and accepted as absolute or I leave myself vulnerable to blaming my lack of success on circumstances and on people I cannot control. If I accept the fact that current frustrations and failures are directly due to my lack of understanding of myself, my team and the people with whom I must relate (customers, vendors, creditors, etc.) I can turn immediately from frustration, fear, accusation and other excuses and begin to solve the problems in front of me.

How is this done? First, if you haven't already, take the Professional Personality Index test and discover your personal index of values, traits and strategies. Then begin in the next chapter to increase your understanding of how to use this new knowledge to improve your performance at work and in your life in general.

Note: For those who are reading this Resource Guide to learn how to teach others to put the Professional Personality Index to practical use, it is essential that you fully participate in the Index testing and practical application in your own life and career. To the degree that you are able to internalize the principles described throughout this Resource Guide, you will be able to communicate this knowledge clearly to others and assist them in applying their growing knowledge to their daily situations.

PROFESSIONAL PERSONALITY INDEX™

Primary Social Values

BUILDER *Action* *Results*	**MERCHANT** *Vision* *Relationships*
BANKER *Conservation* *Information*	**INNOVATOR** *Assessment* *Solutions*

© Copyright Lynn Ellsworth Taylor, November 1997

The Four Basic Personality Styles

In my work as a business management consultant I use every tool available to understand how to unlock the potential and release the energy in struggling and dynamic growth companies. These tools are used to uncover better uses of financial resources, better application of people and to attain new levels of growth and success for stronger companies as well.

One such tool has been the Professional Personality Index™ for business owners, business managers and their teams. The Index divides people into four personality types and combinations thereof. This approach is not new. It has been attempted as far back as Plato and is a significant element in much of the current human resource course work and modern psychology.

But the Professional Personality Index has been designed specifically for contemporary business. The four leadership styles from ancient business practices which have been chosen (Bankers, Merchants, Innovators, and Builders) are ascribed by the things people value and the strategies they use to get what they want.

It is essential to understand our individual leadership strategies and personality styles. This knowledge allows us to better relate to others, to be more effective in getting what we want, and to increase agreement with others who can contribute to our success. All of which insures our ability to succeed in business.

Builders are a well respected group of people, powerful in scope of work, leaders in the creation of lasting monuments to themselves and their civilizations. Builders cause action, make decisions and drive toward results, making concrete the aspirations and innovations of Merchants, Innovators and Bankers. Builders get results.

Merchants were the first sales people, but more than this, they were the risk takers, the visionaries, the traders opening new markets. Those who saw what could be, and energized their societies to pursue wealth and art and beauty. Merchants sell, motivate, inspire and make things happen for Builders, Innovators and Bankers. Merchants are team builders and deal makers.

Innovators constantly add to society through their ability to solve problems, see possibilities and strive toward effective solutions. When others around them claim it can't be done, Innovators ask "What if." Innovators provide solutions to Builders and Merchants and to Bankers. Innovators always find a better way.

Bankers do much more than keep the books, control money and record the past. Some bankers are not involved in these tasks at all. They assimilate all available data. They organize thought and information so that others can be more effective. They challenge the viability of new directions by showing past successes and failures. They keep balance in the system. Bankers keep Merchants, Builders and Innovators from the edges of unreasonable risk. Bankers conserve, analyze and inform.

What kind of Leader are you?

Generally, you will find that you are strongly inclined toward one strategy with a second personality strategy being a very important part of your make-up. You may identify your leadership and personality style best by saying you are a Merchant-Builder, or Innovator-Banker, or Banker-Builder, etc. It is generally more effective to state your dominant personality style first, and your secondary style last.

Whatever your leadership strategy, it is essential that each company and each department within a company contains the talents of each personality style and in the right balance. If any one type of personality is not balanced by the others all of the strengths of a Builder, Merchant, Innovator or Banker become the weaknesses of that person or group of people, and the business will suffer accordingly.

The success of any business manager is based upon the ability to create appropriate balance of human resources within his or her company and to appropriately focus the energies of the personalities toward tasks which they are most likely to perform well. The challenge is that each business has its own unique requirement for a different set of personality and leadership styles.

There is, of course, a corresponding list of negative attributes which go along with each personality (leadership) style. Although I choose to approach life from the positive side most of the time, it is critical that each of us as individuals understand how and when our strengths can become our weaknesses.

I do not need to paint this picture for you in detail. You can do it for yourself. Simply use the lists of words from which you have made your choices and again read down each column of boxes across each row.

If you are primarily a Builder, for instance, look at the word boxes where you have selected the "Builder" word. Now read the words which you did not select in this box, which other personality styles would select. We can focus only on one priority at a time. So, if you begin your assessment of negative attributes with the positive word, "Results," you will notice that while you are focused on results you are not focused on Relationships, Solutions, or Statistics.

The strength of being results-oriented becomes unbalanced when that focus discounts the value of long term relationships, ignores more beneficial solutions and denies the need for information which might lead to consistency. Results may be achieved now but the same job may have to be done over and over again if the required balance is not in place.

Continue this analysis through each box where you selected a word representing your dominant personality style. This will give you a fair idea of the areas which are not strong points and where you tend to defeat your own purposes on occasion. In other words, while you are busy being a Builder you are not busy being a Merchant or an Innovator or a Banker. This fact guarantees an imbalance in three out of four areas at every moment of your life.

The secret to consistent success is knowing when to continue being a Builder because the power of that strategy is creating the success which is desired, and when to shift to a secondary or even minor personality trait in order to be more successful in a new situation or to avoid old patterns that have led to failures in the past.

We professional business people are not as self-sufficient as we would like to think. Those who learn this secret optimize their personal power, build effective teams around them and the capabilities and power of the whole team becomes greater than the sum of its parts.

Some of us are quite reasonably balanced. We are able to utilize a variety of strategies when things are going well. But all of us, when our backs are against the wall, or when we run up against other personality styles that surprise us, collapse back into our emotionally based, fear based strategies. We will almost always revert to our dominant personality style and to its most negative, least effective strategies in these instances.

Some people because of the manner in which they were raised, revert to personality styles which are completely different from their dominant or secondary Index category. Once this fact is understood all of the communication and interactions we are going to be learning in this Resource Guide can be applied equally well to these persons even when in defensive or aggressive postures.

A powerful, successful business leader allows herself to slip into this negative defensive posture only on rare occasions and is quick to recognize and to fix the effects of these momentary lapses. Some of us live in this reactive mode most of the time. This is not a formula for success.

PRIMARY SOCIAL VALUES
BUILDER

Action

Results

© Copyright Lynn Ellsworth Taylor, November 1997

BUILDERS

If you are a Builder, which a significant percentage of business owners and business leaders are, you are successful because you get things done. You take personal responsibility. You don't usually make excuses and you are generally impatient with those who do. You make decisions on the fly and like it that way. Your focus is short term and driven by the sense of accomplishment in the moment.

Builders have an internal drive that allows them to be decisive, to blow through obstacles and make decisions spontaneously. They are constantly turning their energies loose on an identified goal, and are not willing to accept defeat, at least not gracefully.

It is obvious why Builders make good business leaders. Bankers and Merchants and Innovators who have strong secondary Builder characteristics also succeed very well. But before we praise Builders too greatly, let's take a look at a Builder who is trying to operate a company without a balanced team.

Joseph Casper owns a five million dollar high technology company. He has been successful in obtaining contracts with the government and his business has many times been quite profitable. However, after twenty years in business he seems to have reached a dramatic plateau. Actually it was reached six years ago but he is just now admitting that maybe he could use some help.

This is the first weakness of Builder leaders. They try to do everything themselves, are not effective at teaching others, too impatient. And Builders are so focused on getting things done, **right now**, that they typically create an environment of crisis. They thrive as fire fighters. Which is good, since their style of management creates one fire after another.

Builders care more about results than relationships or well conceived, long term solutions. They like to go home tired and hungry. And they like sex after every battle. Builders often confuse taking action with getting an appropriate result.

Mr. Casper can be seen many times each day charging out of his office on a mission. His method of leadership is to command. He has had a thought. He is looking for someone to take that thought and act on it. When he finds a likely candidate he is **not** careful to request attention. He demands it. He seldom waits while his target finishes a phone call or a conversation or a sentence on the computer. He begins speaking sometimes before he enters his target's office.

You will often hear a Builder saying things like:

"Just do it."

"Get out of my way."

"I'll do it."

"Not in my house (yard, family, company, department, etc.)

"Make it happen."

"I don't care what I said yesterday."

Because of the apparent strength of Builders, others tend to not stand up against them, especially when the Builder is the boss, although I have witnessed many companies which are being run by secretaries, bookkeepers, even receptionists because their Builder strategies are being allowed to exert inappropriate control.

PROFESSIONAL PERSONALITY INDEX™

BUILDER: negative traits

- Pushy
- Angry
- Frustrated
- Gruff
- Always Right

- Inconsiderate
- Overbearing
- Arrogant
- Bossy

© Copyright Lynn Ellsworth Taylor, November 1997

Builders, not being highly tuned toward reading the reactions and needs of other humans, barely comprehend that this might be important. Builders are not good team-builders. If a Builder is good at this he is using a secondary Merchant (relationship) strategy or the Innovator (solution) strategy to accomplish the team-building "project." Builders approach team building the way they approach starting their car. "So, turn the key on. Let's get on with it." Builders are not good at foreplay.

Builders value action and results above all other business factors. Their mode of teaching others is to push people out of the way, take the business tool in their own hands and say, "Just watch me do it." They then leave and expect their "student" to be as proficient at the task as the Builder is. Not a "Great Expectation."

Builders often confuse taking an action with getting a result. Although they tend to be very pragmatic people and bottom line oriented, when it comes to their own performance they are so hell bent on taking action that they often forget what their mission is. They loose sight of their objectives in the heat of the moment.

Taking an action feels just as good to Builders as completing a project. Given a command that something be done is a "result" for a Builder. They have experienced their energy, enjoyed the work and feel charged with new energy ready for the next task. They over-look detail, do not often measure effectiveness or results, despise too much information or tracking, are impatient with Innovators who spend too long reasoning out a situation and see Merchants as unreliable airheads.

Builders are impatient with the world, especially Bankers and Merchants and Innovators. In other words no one else's values or considerations are important to a Builder when she is after a specific result or simply wants to take action. Time is always paramount to a Builder. Since Builders consider Merchants "light-weights" and "flakes," and Merchants value relationship so highly, Builders are not good at motivating Merchants.

Builders also have low tolerance for having to give instructions to anyone. They are so motivated and self-sufficient that such instruction appears a total waste (baby-sitting). Since Bankers refuse to take an action without knowing precisely what action to take, Builders do not get the benefit of effective Bankers around them very often. In truth Builders **don't know how** to tell anyone how to do anything. They'd rather get it done themselves.

Builders enjoy Innovators immensely as long as the Builder is boss. Innovators give Builders solutions to problems and Builders are the best implementers around. This relationship feeds the Builder's personal needs very well.

Blowing relationships up is a past time of Builders and has no more import to them than blowing up ideas or disrupting systems that are too comfortable, or just commanding obedience to see if it can be obtained. Since Bankers are risk averse, want to know facts before proceeding and hesitate with every decision, Builders see Bankers as brick walls that regularly need to be blown apart or consigned to the "Back Forty."

PROFESSIONAL PERSONALITY INDEX™

BUILDER: when we are pushed

- Shout
- Get Angry
- Change Our Minds
- Ridicule
- Intimidate
- Bluster
- Stomp Out
- Command
- Attack
- Make You Wrong
- Shame You
- Point the Finger
- Blow Up Friendships
- We Overpower You

© Copyright Lynn Ellsworth Taylor, November 1997

Builders like action, activity, energy, and they will sacrifice relationships, effectiveness, stability to have their energy fix.

Builders are powerful people. They act from their gut and trust their own judgment explicitly. This makes them very decisive. This can be very intimidating to others. In fact intimidation is the Builder's primary way of getting control in any situation. If the sheer power of their personality and decisiveness is not sufficient to maintain control, they will resort to anger, hostility, arm waving, stomping and fuming, threatening reprisal. When a Builder is out of control, only the strong survive in the same room.

PRIMARY SOCIAL VALUES
MERCHANT

Vision

Relationships

© Copyright Lynn Ellsworth Taylor, November 1997

MERCHANTS

Merchants tend to be exceptional team builders. They rally people around, are constantly excited by new ideas and are never the one to ask if something is possible. They assume every idea they have is possible. In fact just having an idea is cause for celebration and reward as far as Merchants are concerned. "Nothing happens without a good idea."

The power of Merchants comes from this willingness to think about, consider and expose one good thought after the next. They think as they speak, changing and modifying their vision in real time. Since every business is a constantly changing organism Merchants are invaluable resources.

Their excitement is infectious and people work better when they feel energized. Unlike Builders, Merchants get little satisfaction from feeling their own energy which is considerable; But Merchants thrive on infecting the world around them with excitement toward the common vision. They not only create teams, they inspire, motivate and direct teams toward real (and sometimes imagined) opportunities.

Merchants also have appreciation for culture, art, literature, quality of presentation, aesthetics. Without the Merchant mind involved in a business the work place becomes a chaotic miasma of Builder verbiage on scratch pads, Banker spreadsheets and reports, and Innovator block diagrams and technical manuals.

Merchants attract others to them, an invaluable asset in business.

Merchants, however, consider themselves God's gifts to humanity. They think highly of themselves and believe everyone loves them. If they didn't believe this they wouldn't get anything done. They are a joy to have around. Merchants, however seldom complete any task. They are great starters, good at foreplay. But without a Builder around to make things happen, and a Banker to keep things from getting out of hand, a Merchant will constantly be stirring up more fish than anyone can catch and landing very few of them.

Merchants also become easily frustrated and don't take rejection well. Innovators have to constantly help Merchants see a new approach, because Merchants tend to think that "being liked" is all that is required. Merchants pout when they perceive they are unappreciated and almost everything a Builder or Banker does makes a Merchant feel unappreciated.

Merchants sell. Whether they are involved in sales as a business function or not, Merchants sell, as much to themselves as to anyone else. Merchants take care of their friends and customers. They nurture long term relationships. In fact they value relationships more than results.

A business owner or business leader who is predominately a Merchant will generate incredible energy and get almost instant rewards. They can't live without some sort of reward (personal feedback, money, idea validation) for longer than ten or fifteen minutes. But the rewards tend to come from many diverse directions and seldom relate to the Merchant's own long term vision. A Merchant is perfectly willing to revise her long term vision as often as required, more often than required.

PROFESSIONAL PERSONALITY INDEX™

MERCHANT: negative traits

- Forgetful
- Flighty
- Inconsistent
- Pouty
- Flippant

- Manipulative
- Exaggerating
- Unfounded
- Impulsive

© Copyright Lynn Ellsworth Taylor, November 1997

Merchants get results, but usually indirectly. Merchants are the ones who help others see opportunity. In fact Merchants see opportunities that aren't even there. Merchants like to start something new as often as possible. If they finish something it's because they don't want to disappoint someone, not because they themselves value completion and results. Being in the game is what feels good to a Merchant.

Business leaders who are predominantly Merchants tend to build well diversified companies. There are very few opportunities that get by them. Without a little Banker sitting on their shoulder to hold them back they can be dangerous. It also helps Merchants to have some Builder characteristics and some Innovator problem solving and strategizing skills. Without this balance they tend to start lots of things, finish nothing and have a hell of a good time doing it— little to show for the effort afterwards.

Merchants tend to succeed quite well at building their teams, but where they fall short is in giving their team members the power to control the Merchant's whims and need for constant stimulation. In order for Merchants to have a strong company or department they have to give someone else considerable right and authority to keep the boss in chains. They need to fulfill their requirement for constant newness and stimulation outside the work place.

"Get a life," as some would say

Because Merchants value vision and relationships above all else they see the future when others are stuck in the past or the crisis in the present. They know how to sell their vision to others and create tremendous energy by exciting others with their ideas. And, contrary to the opinion of Builders, Merchants tend to be quite pragmatic, deriving most of their vision from extrapolating from today's situation.

Their extrapolations are necessarily loose and without detail so Bankers cringe every time the Merchant is loose in the house. But Innovators love being around a Merchant because Innovators love a new problem to solve, a new solution to explore. They fill in the required systems and steps a Merchant may only dimly see, pass on the plan to a Builder. Then while the Builder is taking action and demanding that every one around him also take action on the plan, the Merchant is conceiving another vision, the Innovator is developing another level of complexity and sophistication, perfecting (changing) the plan already at play, and the Banker is still testing the advisability of moving ahead on any of this risky business.

Merchants will often be heard saying:

"Come on. Let's go."

"Let's do it."

"We can do it."

"I'll teach you how."

"Let's work it out."

"This is going to make us rich."

"We are going to get a lot of business out of this."

"Why don't we..."

"Wait and see... You'll believe me then."

"What file?"   *"What appointment?"*
"What report?"

"I thought we did that yesterday."

PROFESSIONAL PERSONALITY INDEX™

MERCHANT: when we are pushed

- Pout
- Whine
- Give Up
- Cajole
- Change the Subject
- Talk About the Future
- Judge You to be Beneath Us
- Discount What You Say
- Attack
- Manipulate
- Exaggerate
- Sell-sell-sell Complain
- Look Innocent
- Throw Up Our Hands
- Cling to Anyone
- We Win You Over

© Copyright Lynn Ellsworth Taylor, November 1997

Merchants act from inspiration, act with energy and thrive on excitement. They hate redundancy, especially in their own patterns of activity. They generally like being watched when they are performing, visioning, teaching, inspiring, but they hate being measured, evaluated, tested, critiqued.

If you succeed in managing Merchants, it is through obtaining their loyalty and their desire to please you for the sake of maintaining their relationship with you. Or you can get them to be practical by holding out the promise that in the future they will be able to see another of their ideas come into play.

When Merchants feel out of control, put upon, or under-valued (un-loved) they have several very effective strategies for getting back into control. They whine, a sound which attracts the attention, sympathy of all other Merchants within earshot. They cajole, manipulate and hang their heads in shame to make you back off.

If all else fails Merchants, when feeling unappreciated, will exaggerate the opportunity or change the subject from present performance to a vision of the future. If you mistreat them (by their standards) they judge you to be beneath them. They keep on selling, never shutting up to let others speak. They look innocent and talk innocent and cling to anyone who looks or sounds supportive.

They will try to love you to death and **win you over**. If that doesn't work they will try to shame you regarding the way you are treating them, making you look evil in the eyes of all observers. Merchants pout until everyone else gives in. Merchants make the best victims. They know the "Poor Me" dramas of life very well. They are great actors.

You can spot the Merchants on a basketball team by discerning their success at getting charging violations called on their opponents.

PRIMARY SOCIAL VALUES
INNOVATOR

Assessment Solutions

© Copyright Lynn Ellsworth Taylor, November 1997

INNOVATORS

Innovators are the solution creators in this world. They can always think of another approach. "There's got to be a better way," is more than their motto; It is a pre-programmed ROM chip in their brain's rectilinear receiver. Innovators enjoy the challenge of a problem. They are problem solvers. They enjoy this so much that they hate to settle on any one solution—"There's got to be an even better way."

The power of Innovators comes from their unwillingness to accept that there is anything they can't figure out. They are willing to put their ego at risk over and over again, staked on the bet that they will be able to come up with a plan, a solution, an idea that will makes things better.

Then to top things off Innovators love to develop systems which insure the continuation of their plans. These systems are the monuments of Innovators, just as much as a pyramid is the monument of a Builder.

When everyone around them is in panic, the Builder shouting orders, the Merchant whining or up-selling and the Banker preaching justice or patience, the Innovator tends to isolate, grab a computer or white board and set quietly to work.

They are highly creative in their approach to problem solving, always able to come at things from a new angle, adding elements, systems and technologies that no one else has thought to add into the mix, in order to achieve a sound innovation.

While the solutions and systems that Innovators create are well founded and practical in concept, Innovators themselves are not highly practical in approach. They do not make good implementers because they want to perfect everything before acting and taking action to them is coming up with another innovation which delays one more time the implementation of their systems or new products.

Innovators love to have people around. This is not team-building. This is an audience for their creativity. They love to explore their latest ideas with people. They are so fascinated with each personally conceived 'potential' solution that they want everyone to appreciate each and every subtlety. Just when they have their audience convinced that this solution is brilliant they love to add, "Wait, what if we...?"

Innovators sometimes create problems just for the pleasure of working them out.

Builders lean on Innovators but often leave them standing in the hallway half way through an explanation about a possible solution. Banker's constantly feed challenges to an Innovator's proposed strategy, keeping the Innovator charged with new problems to face. Merchants listen attentively to Innovators and lean on them constantly. This makes the Innovator feel "heard," and since the Merchant would never consider leaving an Innovator standing in the hallway Innovators and Merchants often become great friends. Their brainstorming parties are endless; If unmanaged, an endless drain of company resources.

Innovators are invaluable. They create new products, put together systems to solve production and administrative problems. They are never defeated, able to come up with new strategies and approaches when everyone has given up. They enjoy this so much they hate making decisions, and they constantly add confusion to the system by always

PROFESSIONAL PERSONALITY INDEX™
INNOVATOR: negative traits

- Stubborn
- Distracted
- Disconnected
- Uncooperative
- Unresponsive
- One Track Mind
- Indecisive
- Protected
- Cool

© Copyright Lynn Ellsworth Taylor, November 1997

THE FOUR BASIC PERSONALITY STYLES

inventing a better way. Nothing is ever good enough, especially if it was conceived by someone else or if the solution has been in place for more than a few nano-seconds.

Business owner Innovators can be highly successful. They are the people that create the mouse trap that brings the world to their door. The problem is they really believe that this will happen. And since they love the process of problem solving more than the process of actually building and selling something, as soon as one product or service idea is implemented, they are off to create another better solution.

The more deadly sin of Innovators is their desperate need to continue perfecting a product or system long after it would fully serve its purpose. They get addicted to working on a specific solution.

Recently I was introduced to a software company which was being run by two Innovators, both with secondary Builder traits. These two had devised a very clever software program which they had released but not yet de-bugged. Each time a "bug" was reported to the company one of these two would grab the "bug" project and set out to correct it, making numerous innovations in the process, and not considering any of the ramifications related to existing customers, changes required in the manuals or profits.

When asked to stop innovating, and "just fix the bugs," They said they would try but later admitted that they would probably never do that. "As long as I'm inside the code I might as well fix everything." The problem is their fixes tended to create additional problems for them and for others. Innovators cannot leave well enough alone.

They desperately needed a Banker to come in and detail their programs, finding and fixing without making additional changes. But the Innovators say, "No one will ever be able to understand the clever things we have done. We can't trust anyone else with the source code."

Interestingly, whenever one of them comes into the office with a new set of innovations and a "bug" fix, they turn their Builder personality loose and demand that everyone instantly convert their fixes to product, get it packaged and out the door, causing no end of chaos and frustration. This is an ineffective use of their Builder characteristics.

Active Innovators need a Builder in them or around them to insist that they settle on one solution and complete it. They need Merchants who will actually make someone else understand the value of the "solution" being sold. And they need Bankers who will support them by completing the details and help them control costs and make profits.

Innovators are very stubborn people. They refuse to be moved until they feel their solutions are perfected. And since they also value assessment very highly, they not only like to create a new solution, but they want to be the one who assesses its appropriateness, its correctness, its cleverness, its perfection. In fact they are certain that no one else could ever understand all the subtlety and complexity of their solution so they hate to let others really get into it and explore.

Every decision for an Innovator becomes a marathon of adding one more consideration into the equation, testing its full ramifications and announcing that "I can see how that will fit." Then

PROFESSIONAL PERSONALITY INDEX™
INNOVATOR: when we are pushed

- Re-route
- Get Stubborn
- Re-compute
- Try to Confuse You with the Facts
- Complicate Your Life
- Withhold Feelings
- Re-consider
- Shut Down
- Slow You Down
- Deny Facts That Don't Fit Our Solutions
- We Quit!

© Copyright Lynn Ellsworth Taylor, November 1997

when everyone else considers the decision to have been made the Innovator announces another level of considerations which must be explored prior to finalizing the decision. Innovators can be infuriating to Merchants and Builders who want to move on.

Innovators will often be heard saying:

"I think I can make that work."

"We can do that."

"It's not ready yet."

"When I say it's finished, it's finished."

"All we have left to do is..."

"There's got to be a better way."

"These things are never finished."

"Wait. What if we...?"

But Innovators are very perceptive. They see and understand the tensions they cause and they are willing to act differently if they can only see how the different action is going to produce better results. For this reason, Innovators and Builders make wonderful team mates. They tend to keep good balance in the drive for action versus the drive for perfection.

The adaptiveness of Innovators is also highly prized by all other players. Innovators make little distinction between what problem they are asked to solve. The process of deriving a solution is sufficient to make them happy. So, Innovators are a key element in every business situation where change is occurring. Their resourcefulness brings new methods, new tools, new systems, new mechanisms to bear, always opening new opportunity for success.

An opposite tendency is also true for many Innovators. They tend to become highly skilled at solving certain types of problems. Innovator Engineers, for instance, may be geniuses when designing a new electronic circuit but more like absent minded professors when it comes to developing business solutions for their departments.

When Innovators are out of control they get stubborn. They look for another way, the way to go around you, to make you re-consider. They reconsider and resist making a decision. They FUME and refuse to talk about it. They stare you down with a stare that says, "How can you be so stupid?" They add another wrinkle to the equation to confuse you. They deny facts, challenge the validity of data (This really infuriates Bankers). They refuse to take action which puts Builders into a rage. They quit, popping the balloons of the Merchant on their way out.

When all else fails, Innovators resort to interrogation. They like to confuse the issue with side questions. They know how to ask questions which are more accusation than question. They know how to get under the skin of other people, asking questions that shame and embarrass, that show the ignorance of others or simply make others feel ignorant or confused and inadequate. Interrogation is just as powerful a strategy as the intimidation of Builders, the Poor Me, victim caretaking role of the Merchants or the aloof, resistant, judgmental unchangeable positioning of the Bankers.

PRIMARY SOCIAL VALUES
BANKER

Information

Conservation

Analysis

© Copyright Lynn Ellsworth Taylor, November 1997

BANKERS

Bankers have the hardest time as small business owners. This is because they are most effective in an environment that needs quantification, that needs management of complex, effective systems, that needs balance and information. In the early stages of company development, until a company reaches $5.0 to $10.0 million in annual sales, Bankers tend to over-organize, over-correct and generally over-manage everything. In fact this is always their tendency.

The power of Bankers is in their clear mindedness. They are organized to the last degree. Data is at their finger tips and they don't miss details. Bankers are insatiable information gathers. They are like magnets dragged through sand, collecting all the valuable shards of fact. This information becomes a base of knowledge and expertise which has an intrinsic value, a marketable worth. Bankers become part of the asset base of the Companies they serve because of their industry and technical knowledge or service expertise.

Once gathered, the information is ordered, assimilated and reproduced in a manner which leaves nothing out. Because all details are critical to Bankers they are not good at setting priorities, becoming a wealth of information for others who wish to explore their library-like minds.

Bankers are committed to assuring that whatever is done is successful. They are adamant about not launching the ship before its sea-worthiness has been tested. Whenever I ride in an airplane I am thankful for the Banker minds in the FAA. When I take pills to help recover from an illness I appreciate the Banker minds in the FDA.

It is those same Banker minds in the FAA and FDA which so infuriate businesses who want to launch their products.

Without Banker influence in any situation, actions are taken without sufficient thought, directions are changed without considering long term ramifications or bottom-line consequences and new innovations are put into play without regard to service problems, system failures and customer satisfaction.

Bankers, more than any of the other personality types, tend to find themselves standing alone, holding their position in order to effect their most important purpose— to conserve resources, insure longevity and stabilize the business or society they are in.

Bankers frustrate Builders immensely. The results orientation and decisiveness of a Builder is the opposite of a Banker's mentality. Bankers also frustrate Merchants but more typically are themselves frustrated by Merchants. The constant stirring up of opportunity and the typical lack of value of Merchants on completion of projects, lack of concern for details keeps Bankers constantly feeling under-informed and off balance, two feelings Bankers despise.

Bankers get along quite well with Innovators since Innovators have a high level of regard and need for the information which Bankers horde. Information and solutions fit together nicely. And Bankers serve Innovators well by providing much needed analysis and accrued information which keep the Innovator on track and confident of the solutions being implemented.

PROFESSIONAL PERSONALITY INDEX™
BANKER: negative traits

- Cold
- Unmoving
- Always Right
- Judgemental
- Myopic
- Indecisive
- Withholding
- Reticent

© Copyright Lynn Ellsworth Taylor, November 1997

A Banker who has strong Merchant characteristics or strong Innovator or Builder traits can succeed admirably as a leader in a new enterprise. They must be willing, however, to keep their own dominant Banker trait in check until there is truly a need for it in the business.

Since Bankers are like Builders in their in-attention to team building they very often try to control their companies or their departments personally far too long. They are detail oriented people concerned with knowing where everything is. Preservation is more important to them than creation. The role of a business owner is to create something out of nothing. This is the antithesis of a Banker's spirit.

Bankers, as much as any other personality style, must have strong partners or employees who provide the creative energy, the sales, the team-building and the drive to get results. They just don't like to admit it.

Bankers don't like to stop counting things and making sure all information is in, any more than Innovators like to stop thinking of solutions. A Banker will seldom make a decision except by omission or delay. Note: It is important to draw a distinction between saying "No," which means "Nothing is going to change," and making a decision which dictates change and which therefore increases risk. Bankers are good at saying "No."

The power of a Banker as a business leader comes from the Banker's hatred of waste and distaste for risk. Once a Banker is placed into a high risk situation, where resources are limited, his drive to get back into a secure position may cause the Banker to rely more heavily on the Merchants, Innovators or Builders around him. This drive to create something solid and resistant to outside pressures, makes a successful Banker's company recession-proof, and highly resilient, seldom under-capitalized.

Bankers who are acting out of their strengths are invaluable.

Without a Banker personality in any sales department, production shop, marketing office, the number of repetitive mistakes buries the business. Opportunities are lost, orders are misplaced and forgotten. Shipment schedules are considered a nuisance. Bankers are unwilling to be part of an operation that doesn't fulfill its commitments. They will do almost anything to make things right.

The analytical power of a Banker far exceeds that of the other personality types. When serious problems arise a Banker becomes an essential resource. She has collected information by sheer will and desire and is able to deliver this information in a clear and balanced form. A Banker will take the solutions presented by an Innovator and formulate the solution down to the task level, understanding the interrelationship of all elements.

And the final answers that come from a Banker are solid. They are a long time coming, but when they do arrive they are solid.

When a Banker gets pressed, pushed to the wall, forced to make a decision or act against his analytical conclusions, he will simply disengage, back out. Bankers judge others as being wrong, and withdraw their trust. They will withhold information to regain control. And they will use that information to undermine others when the opportunity arises.

PROFESSIONAL PERSONALITY INDEX™

BANKER: when we are pushed

- Back Out
- Play Victim or Judge
- Talk About the Past
- Promise
- Pretend Capitulation
- Say No, No, No
- Re-organize, Re-analyze
- Politic
- Passive Aggressive
- Undermine
- Criticize
- Judge Our Own Imperfection
- We Outlast You

© Copyright Lynn Ellsworth Taylor, November 1997

Because they dislike conflict, Bankers will make promises they do not intend to keep, or they will simply say a flat, unqualified "No" to everything, hoping that this simple act will be powerful enough to cause others to draw back and surrender. When Bankers feel out of control they become aloof, untouchable, unreasonable, intractable, non-responsive, unavailable, busy.

Bankers will always outlast Builders, Merchants and Innovators in a battle because they refuse to invest any energy in the battle until everyone else is exhausted. Then they make their play.

Some of the things you will hear Bankers say are:

"No. Can't be done."

"Get out of my face (space)."

"Go ahead, if you really have to."

"I told you..."

"I'm studying that right now."

"Not with my money."

"We've never done it that way before."

"Even if we succeed, it won't be enough."

Bankers have extraordinary staying power. Their compulsion to be right or to be seen as being right does not allow them to admit failure; So they keep trying, keep doing, keep analyzing until often, by perseverance alone, they succeed where others would have failed long before.

PROFESSIONAL PERSONALITY INDEX™: Basis For Success

BUILDER
Gut Level
Decisive
Powerful

MERCHANT
Inspired
Energized
Exciting

INTUITIVE

BANKER
Analytical
Formulative
Solid

INNOVATOR
Perceptive
Adaptive
Resourceful

COGNITIVE

© Copyright Lynn Ellsworth Taylor, November 1997

THE FOUR BASIC PERSONALITY STYLES

COMMON TRAITS

Each of the personality styles has some traits in common with the other types of personalities. It is important to note these common traits because each person has a dominant and secondary index. The character traits which exist in both a dominant and secondary personality style of an individual may not have balancing traits which off-set the strengths inherent in the common traits. These strengths are then more likely to become over-riding weakness.

Merchants and Builders, for instance, are **intuitive** in their thinking. Builders tend to act from the gut, from impulse. Merchants, also intuitive, act from inspiration, both of which traits are spontaneous. So, Merchants and Builders tend to act without a lot of thought or second guessing. They tend to make quick decisions based upon the way things **feel**. They both believe in their capacity to know what to do next, so planning is not crucial.

On the opposite side of the fence are the Innovators and Bankers. They are **cognitive** in their thought processes and make decisions based upon assessment (Innovators) or analysis (Bankers). These people are slower to decide what to do and tend to question what they are doing as they go. They make decisions based upon what they **think or know** versus what they feel. They are therefore not good decision makers, at least not quick decision makers.

Bankers and Builders share the common trait of being "right." These people are never wrong. Builders are never wrong because they are acting from the gut, and who can challenge the validity of a gut instinct? Bankers are never wrong because they have the data to back up their actions and conclusions. They can prove they are right if you are intelligent enough to understand their proof. Bankers and Builders are never wrong and will be happy to make you wrong anytime you choose to disagree with them.

Bankers and Builders also are practical in nature, believe in implementation and doing. Innovators and Merchants, on the other hand, tend to be creative, believe in innovation and teaching others. Neither Bankers nor Builders make good teachers, Builders because of their impatience and "Watch me" attitude, Bankers because of their step by step, black and white approach to life which only registers with other Bankers.

Innovators and Merchants share the trait of needing to be valued, to be seen as being good. Merchants tend to believe that God is on their side and that their goodness assures them of being loved, being wealthy and keeping friends. Innovators have a similar value in their solutions, in the beauty of their creations, in the cleverness of their systems. Innovators believe they are irreplaceable, valuable and doing good for society. Merchants and Innovators tend to dismiss others because others are beneath them in value and goodness.

Merchants and Bankers are at far ends of the spectrum in their approach to most of life. However in one area they share a strong shared character trait. They both tend to view their value systems as the highest and best. Bankers value justice and measure all actions and people by the Banker's sense of justice. Merchants value love and relationships and measure actions and people by

PROFESSIONAL PERSONALITY INDEX™
BASIS FOR SUCCESS

BUILDER

Action

Doing

Practicality

Implementation

Information

BANKER

MERCHANT

Vision

Teaching

Innovation

Creativity

Solutions

INNOVATOR

© Copyright Lynn Ellsworth Taylor, November 1997

their contribution to love and relationships (according to the Merchant's definition of good relationships and love).

Merchants and Bankers, therefore try to control not only the actions of others but the manner and means of the actions, the tone of voice, the level of anger, etc. Merchants and Bankers judge others harshly and withdraw if they perceive either injustice (Bankers) or lack of love (Merchants). Bankers are quick to judge and quick to withdraw. Merchants are far more tolerant and tend to be without boundaries with other people, at least until they feel abused or feel their trust has been broken. Once that happens Merchants are the most unforgiving of all personality styles.

Innovators and Builders share the common trait of monument building. Builders like to leave monuments demonstrating their powerful presence on earth in brick and stone and tangible materials. Innovators love to leave their monuments in the form of systems and new products, innovations. In their drive to create monuments to themselves Innovators and Builders often discount the worth of others as being impractical and of little value. Innovators and Builders, after all, create things. What do the others do?—think and dream, study and report. Builders and Innovators are not always great supporters of Merchants and Bankers.

Everybody around me

already knows

my ineffective behaviors.

I might as well talk

about them all

up front and honestly.

© Copyright Lynn Ellsworth Taylor, November 1997

4

The Six Primary Personality Combinations

1. MERCHANT/BUILDERS (BUILDER/MERCHANTS)

When the situation calls for someone who will role up his sleeves and get to work, always keeping high quality relationships and the long term vision in mind, a Merchant/Builder is the best personality for the job. If decisiveness, energy, heart, enthusiasm, strength, openness, spontaneity, are also required, the Merchant/Builder is unbeatable.

These people know how to work and how to get others to work with them. The Builder in them is a doer, and if there is too much work for one person, the Merchant in them will motivate and teach others to perform well. This valuable combination of action aligned with vision, doing aligned with training, results aligned with solid relationships creates an irresistible force.

The action creates worth, the vision creates excitement, the teaching releases new energy and expands capabilities, the decisiveness generates bottom-line results, the care for relationships builds trust and loyalty, the practicality demands respect and the creativity builds appreciation and value.

Merchant/Builders are not good in isolation. They need people around; the Builder side requiring someone to show and command, the Merchant side needing an audience and someone with whom to share the vision and all related successes and failures. Merchants also like to teach, which for them is part of their monument building— the passing along of knowledge and worth, the building of quality relationships which in turn will build more relationships.

So, if building a team rapidly is required, if opening a new sales territory is the task at hand, if a new business enterprise is being launched a Merchant/Builder is the most likely candidate to succeed.

Merchant\Builders, however, tend to believe their own B.S. and all too often fall in love with their own ideas, take dramatic action and leave a trail of bodies and disappointment behind them. They create an incredibly fallow field for Innovators to play in and an endless orgasmic vacuum of fact and balance for a Banker to set straight. Merchant\Builders are socially schizophrenic. One moment they are cajoling and joking and inspiring, then without batting an eye may switch to blustering dynamos of demand. "Just do it," they command.

I have witnessed a Merchant\Builder make one decision, set a course of action, be challenged by her team, deny responsibility, change her mind, set a new course of action, charge the team with a requirement for results and take off on a new idea all within the course of a few sentences and never miss a beat.

These people are explosive and exciting to be around; but if you have a weak heart, avoid them the way people with pace-makers avoid micro-waves. And if you have thin skin, wear a 35 sun-block. Damage control is a necessary task for all the members of a Merchant\Builder's team.

A strong Merchant/Builder can get you to do things you don't like to do and make you believe you're happy doing it.

2. Builder/Innovators (Innovator/Builders)

Business situations which require lasting structures or systems to be built must have Builder/Innovator power at the helm. Whether the requirement is to make something that is complex simple, or to take a simple system and make it more robust and responsive to current needs, the Builder/Innovator is the person for the job.

Builder/Innovators conceive appropriate solutions and take immediate action. Implementing a solution to a problem is a rich form of reward for the Builder, and seeing a system put into effect is the highest praise for an Innovator. So, in the Builder/Innovator we have a person who designs a monument and then builds it.

These powerful personalities are good in isolation. They thrive on independence and chafe under someone else's management. If given a general idea of the problem to be solved or the monument to build, they will find a way to get it done; But give them their head and stand back. Without an open range to work in their energy turns from creativity and action to clever evasion of restrictions, anger and invisibility.

"Where is she?" and "What is he doing now?" are questions often asked of Builder/Innovators by the people around them.

Builder/Innovators are not intimidated by much of anything except intimate relations and speaking to crowds. They are resourceful, agile, constantly in motion, clever, inventive, able to teach others (Innovator), powerful in command (Builder). They derive their own solutions and put them into action without hesitation.

In rapidly changing environments, failing situations, extreme growth opportunities Builder/Innovators are unbeatable.

Builder/Innovators are the answer to every question and the power that can do anything. Their Innovator personality develops one irrefutably valid solution after the next and the Builder in them either pushes everyone out of the way, while they implement the plan, or they pronounce their edict, "Just get it done;"— often adding, "If you can't do it, I'll get someone who can."

Since Builders are impatient with the world, they consider any teaching time to be "baby-sitting." Builder/Innovators are convinced they are self-sufficient. Since they are impatient they also do not have time to be taught or challenged so their ideas are generally the only ones with any merit. Beware of Builder/Innovators. They think Merchants are "airheads" and Bankers are "Little old women, with no spine." (Note: Women who are Builder/Innovators think Bankers and Merchants are "Little old men with no..."

3. Banker/Builders (Builder/Bankers)

Businesses that require high levels of detail, have a high volume of transactions, or have their basis in technical knowledge must have Banker/Builders in leadership. The Banker's commitment to thorough knowledge, to being right, to follow-through and detail is invaluable in these situations. And the ability to take appropriate actions and make decisions in the midst of massive data and volumes of statistics and regulations draw on the strengths of the Builder.

Banker/Builders are tough people to get around. They are self-assured and motivated toward excellence; both in practical results and in legal and moral appropriateness. They tend to set a course and hold to it and do whatever is required to make certain they are able to do so.

Banker/Builders take risks that are well considered and backed by sound reason and fact. These people run well organized beta test sites for new products or take firm leadership in professional service companies such as CPA firms, Attorney partnerships and mutual funds.

Banker/Builders present themselves as masters in their field, as they often are. They tend to be well-educated, speak from knowledge, make demands of others which fit both the person and the situation.

When a Banker/Builder completes a task it has usually been completed on time, under-budget and with excellent attention to quality. Banker/Builders build efficient, practical, durable, financially solvent operations. They are not willing to do less.

Banker/Builders can be arrogant S.O.B.'s who have a great deal of trouble building a team around them. What the Builder in them is not able to make happen can be immediately explained by the statistics and information generated by the Banker side of the personality. These people are never wrong. They don't value Merchants and are impatient with Innovators, and they themselves tend to be very erratic. The Builder makes quick decisions, then back-pedals based upon a new understanding of information, usually derived from Banker driven computer files reviewed at home while other people are sleeping.

Banker/Builders are so certain they are right, they don't bother to gain consensus for their actions or check to see whether anyone else is enjoying the business process. These people burn the energies of others either through erratic commands or stubborn refusal to make a decision. They are known for making a decision one day and remaking it the next, each time with a forceful command for absolute, unquestioning obedience from the team.

Banker/Builders are so self-assured and so unwilling to be wrong that they over-power others around them. These people are more likely to find a way to "run" the business from second and third level positions than any other personality type.

When a Banker/Builder is right in his conclusions he is a powerful steady force that creates firm and unwavering forward motion. When wrong, the Banker/Builder is a belligerent, immovable force willing to make every challenge of his perfection or authority a battle to the death.

And, since there is never a doubt about his own conclusions on the part of the Banker/Builder it is impossible for Merchants and Innovators to know when to go to battle with the Banker/Builder. He is so certain of his knowledge and so comfortable with his compulsion to act that he can get away with murder if that is the action he chooses to take.

4. Merchant/Innovators (Innovator/Merchants)

The power of a Merchant/Innovator derives from her inexhaustible well of creativity. This creates a deep sense of optimism. If the Merchant's dream is not being realized, the Innovator can kick in and come up with appropriate solutions. When the Innovator's solutions do not align perfectly with the Merchant's vision a new vision is deftly formed which can encompass the solutions and systems which the Innovator has conceived and still accomplish all of the basic values foreseen and desired by the Merchant/Innovator.

This constant creativity makes the Merchant/Innovator an invaluable resource in companies where technologies are changing rapidly or competition puts new demands on the marketing and sales systems of the company. Merchant/Innovators are often chosen as sales representatives. They can sell anything because they build relationships and they understand their products and how to make them fit into a broad range of customer situations.

Merchant/Innovators are not put off by any problem of any magnitude. In fact their sense of personal esteem is often based in the size, oppressiveness and worthiness of the problems they have before them. They look for opportunities to demonstrate their prowess at problem solving or at turning around difficult relationships which are at risk.

Merchant/Innovators need to be needed, either for their solutions and technologies or for their humanity, creativity and love. This need to be needed drives them to achieve long term relationships and to develop products and systems which insure the longevity of the relationships which are formed.

Merchant/Innovators are go anywhere, do anything kind of people. They are even able to function for extended periods of time in remote somewhat isolated situations as long as the sense of connection and personal worth is maintained for the Merchant side of the personality. For the Innovator the absorption into the problem solving aspects of any assignment will carry her a long way, as long as there remains an opportunity to observe others evaluating and appraising their work once it is finished.

Merchant/Innovators, despite their ability to sustain themselves independently, thrive best in a team environment. They are excellent team builders and the best teachers. They not only are good at planning a curriculum and basing it in logic and reasonableness but they pay attention to environment, entertainment, energy levels and motivation, creating exciting and provocative learning situations.

A Merchant/Innovator can be an incredible sales person, a powerful business owner, if he is balanced with just enough Builder characteristics to actually complete something. Merchant/Innovators, unrestrained, are a danger to themselves and society. The Merchant is constantly thinking of new projects, new adventures and the Innovator lives off of such challenges.

Innovators hate to bring the process of problem solving to a close. Solving problems is their highest form of pleasure, valuing this game above sex and movies. So a Merchant/Innovator keeps new things coming and keeps everything that was stirred up before "in the works." If you are a Merchant/Innovator, be certain you are surrounded by high energy Builders who will tell you to "Get it done," and a few level headed Bankers who will occasionally ask "Are you serious?"

Merchant/Innovators are constantly caught up in the seduction of a new idea. The concept of a new bridge and the strategy to create it, is more important than the bridge itself. These persons as company leaders never quit selling, never quit solving the future. They sell themselves and others even when everyone has already agreed. There is little attention to detail, and the next new idea takes 110% of all energy so things are constantly left up in the air. Merchant/Innovators tend to be able to keep so much energy swirling around them that they attract others. Builders and Bankers enjoy a symbiotic relationship for a while.

But Merchant/Innovators create as much disappointment as they do opportunity and no one wins from working with them for long, unless there are significant restraints in place and a strong team of Builders and Bankers around them.

If you are a Merchant/Innovator, and you are reading this, you must have just a little Builder or Banker in you. Make sure you nurture that part of yourself—NOW!!!!!

5. Merchant/Bankers (Banker/Merchants)

The worth of Merchant/Bankers is best seen in situations that require highly technical or profuse knowledge to be disseminated to others, or situations in which the demand for risk is high and the need for detail and follow-through extreme. Merchants handle risk very well and Bankers are always considering how they will survive catastrophe. Merchant/Bankers, therefore, are able to play the edge of risk better than any other personality style and survive the experience.

Since the Merchant impulse is to dream and head toward a brighter future, the balance in the Merchant/Banker can be an immense asset. The Banker nature will constantly be looking for ways to assure longevity, survivability, cash strength. And the Merchant's inspired activity will be modulated to a more rational set of activities by the Banker mind, making this personality one which sets many things in motion, completing them all to near perfection.

The Merchant/Banker's capacity to keep many balls in the air and to develop unmatched staying power, assures these persons of staying at play longer than others, being able to go after more opportunities and have something to show for it in the end.

When long term relationships and long term results are the desired outcome, a Merchant/Banker in leadership will provide maximum assurance of a positive outcome.

Merchant/Bankers are also prone to social schizophrenia. When they shift into their Merchant role they are charming, visionary and full of energy. They tend to be a surprise to the people around them, because in business they often bury their Merchant characteristics for fear of being perceived as silly, or unprofessional.

If they allow themselves to be promoters at work, they will often make announcements around new plans and visions on one day and come back the next as their own worst enemy, the Banker in them playing the role of devil's advocate. This sends no small amount of confusion into the team. Merchant/Bankers will tend to be impatient to get things moving, but then direct everyone around them to satisfy the Banker's need for having total information and validation. They may come up with great ideas but they will sabotage these ideas constantly with their own demand to have perfect proof of application.

Cliff, the idiosyncratic story-teller on the TV sitcom "Cheers" is a good example of a poorly performing Merchant/Banker. He has gleaned and garnered thousands of bits of information, some highly interesting and thrown them in with a million bits of fact that no one else cares about. Then his Merchant takes over and demands the spot-light, displaying his knowledge as though on stage, seeking to entertain and impress the multitudes. He is the epitome of a Merchant/Banker at his worst.

Merchant/Bankers tend to be angry or indecisive one day and solicitous, inspiring actions the next. Anger comes from the Banker which expects perfection in implementation and solicitation comes from the Merchant who doesn't want to look like an angry person, for fear that all of her friends may go away.

Merchant/Bankers are fun to watch from a distance but can be hell to work for or live with.

6. Banker/Innovators (Innovator/Bankers)

Banker/Innovators are rationally based, working from fact and provable systems and logical flow. This personality type can rapidly assess a situation and come up with multiple solutions or systems to support the stated objectives. Once conceived the ideas are analyzed, organized, proven on paper and perfected in documentation.

Any business that needs creative solutions in a highly demanding, practical situation will appreciate the contributions of a Banker/Innovator. When the situation calls for reduction of good concepts to design and then the further reduction to documentation and quality control, the Banker/Innovator becomes irreplaceable.

The power of Banker/Innovators in areas of product or system design echo the strengths just discussed for the Merchant/Banker in risky business situations. The Banker/Innovator is prone to push the technological or systems horizons as the Innovator struggles to create the best possible end product while the Banker half of the personality is constantly worrying the details, picking up the unfinished and unresolved design flaws, challenging each step before and after it occurs, assuring maximum likelihood of success.

Banker/Innovators, therefore, are the most likely personality type to push the limits of new product or system development, coming up with true innovations that actually work. There is nothing more valuable to an engineering design team than unlimited innovation balanced by the ability to design such an innovation to perfection and end up with documentation that carries all the way through production, test, pilot manufacturing runs and quality assurance. This same capability is also invaluable in designing new sales processes or in the conception of new service contracts.

It is my suspicion that Calls and Puts in the stock brokerage arena were developed by Banker/Innovators.

Banker/Innovators, however, have a difficult time making decisions. Saying "no" without thought is not making a decision. Information provides evidence to create new solutions, and new solutions need proof which can only be derived from further information, making the process loop endless. If you are a Banker/Innovator and the president of a company (head of a department), God help you and your employees. Your only means to success is through attracting Merchants and Builders with strong enough personalities to act on their own authority and not wait for you to make a decision. They also must be willing to tell you that some of the information you "need" is **not** required in order to get things done.

When Banker/Innovators go into their "no decision today" lock-up, there is no way to get them out of it. The Innovator side gets stubborn and isolates from others until "I can figure this out," and the Banker side sets into motion a protracted data gathering and analysis cycle which "Only I can manage." This posture is impenetrable, unless a courageous Builder simply puts herself at risk and takes unauthorized action and the Merchant stays in the resulting fracas to help resolve relationships and keep everyone focused on the corporate goals.

Try to get a Banker/Innovator to commit a spontaneous action and you will be attempting the impossible. Even Merchants don't envision that ever happening, at least not more than once in a lifetime.

Achieving Company Balance

Every position, every function in every company has a requirement for a unique "optimum" personality profile. And each department in each unique company has an optimum balance of personality and leadership qualities. For instance, a sales department made up of strong Merchant types will be great at stirring up a lot of business but poor at closing, lousy at collecting marketing and sales data, and not good at assimilating new projects and developing new sales approaches. Without strong Builder traits for closing, Banker traits for tracking and reporting and controlling expenses, without Innovator traits to develop new sales promotions and competitive strategies, any sales department will be ineffective.

It is amazing how simple bringing balance into a company or a department can be once all of the players are Indexed according to their Professional Personalities and the related strategies and weaknesses and imbalances are identified.

Good luck. Remember 95% of your time should be spent working on improving and managing your own personality and leadership style. Trust others to make their own progress once their Index is completed and understood. You can't change other people but you can learn to be more effective in your relationships with them. You can learn to dispatch people toward important company objectives based upon their personality index which predicts their likelihood of success in the roles assigned far better than historic resumes.

5

Everything You Always Wanted to Know About Why You Act the Way You Do, But Were always Too Smart to Ask.

We act the way we do because of the mix of two major factors, our genetic disposition to be a Builder, Merchant, Innovator or Banker, and this pre-disposition combined with the environment in which we were raised— Mother was a Builder. Father was a Banker. And I'm a Merchant— which combination required certain survival skills, certain strategies and tactics in order to survive, in order to obtain some comfort and sense of worth.

This interplay between our predisposition toward a personality style and the personality styles (whether highly functional or dysfunctional) of our parents (including other adult and sibling influences) create what some have called a personal Drama. We each have an expected pattern of responses which we are prepared to excite whenever we experience an expected stimulus from others. To really break these patterns many people need to explore the dramas in their family of origin with considerable detail and with the help of counseling professionals. We all have been a little (or a lot) warped out of our natural dispensations by these dramas.

As adults in the business community we tend to surround ourselves with people who keep us in our Drama. Why? Because we have survived and managed this far with our personal strategies and tactics and intend to continue doing so unless the emotional pain or social price becomes too high. It is the known way of behaving which has kept us somewhat safe, warm enough and dry enough thus far.

There is, however, another way to live. We can intentionally set out to discover our personality make-up and to uncover the realities of our personal dramas. This information provides us the basic information we need to begin exploring other more effective strategies for getting the things we truly want.

Most of us are not clear about what we truly want, nor are we willing to believe that we could obtain these things even if we try. Along the way each of us has been undermined and disappointed by circumstances and people. These previous experiences required certain survival techniques which we now re-energize anytime it feels like the old circumstances and disappointments are coming our way.

In business it is critical to provide at least an elementary level of this kind of information so that groups of people can together improve their performance. Employees caught up in personal dramas are forever distracting, undermining, under-performing, carrying low expectations for themselves and the performance of others. The Professional Personality Index is designed to provide immediate stimulus to help people begin breaking these ineffective cycles of poor performance.

Unlike many tests and people-evaluating processes, the Professional Personality Index is designed to be performed by the individual, the results made fully available to the participant and everyone else in the work environment, intentionally avoiding categorizations of people in terms of medical, clinical or psychological classifications.

We each know that we act out in certain ways, that we frustrate ourselves and others by the strategies we choose to solve our problems. The truth is that everyone around us knows and sees our ineffective behaviors. They also see our strengths and special talents. We might as well talk about them all, up front and honestly.

When I know, that you know, that I know that the behavior patterns I continue to use are just as frustrating and disappointing to me as they are to you, we suddenly have an objective and clean way to talk about how to improve my performance and our relationship. We may even find a way to talk about your performance and how you can contribute better to our common goals.

The Four Horses of Ben Hur

According to the wonderful classic movie, when Ben Hur was training his four horses for the chariot races in Rome, he arranged the four white beauties according to their basic natures: The steady, tireless one on the inside,- next to her, the strong, powerful worker— accompanied by the passionate high energy, slightly out of control fury— and on the outside the course correcting, balancing force, the versatile stallion.

This is the kind of balance a good manager or business owner seeks to create, making certain that the other horses around her make an excellent balance for her own unique personality style.

Smart business people use every tool available to measure, evaluate, assess and bring into the light of open discussion the strengths, weaknesses, attributes and ineffectiveness of every member of every team.

Much of my job as a business transition manager is ascribed to the process of creating visibility, making every business issue apparent, measurable and clear to all players. I find that by telling people the truth about what is required, about what is actually happening and about what their contribution is, versus what it must be—everyone immediately begins to find ways to either hide or improve. Most choose to improve, or if they are unable, they ask for training, new skills or a better understanding of what is expected.

Give the Professional Personality Index test to everyone on your team and turn them loose on the project of assessing the effectiveness of each person as related to company goals. I know you will be surprised and gratified with the results.

Note: For most people it takes a failed business, loss of a job, divorce, or emotional trauma to get them to look seriously at the subconscious patterns which control their lives. The Professional Personality Index is not meant to be taken this far, but may serve for many as a significant step toward better self-knowledge and therefore the impetus to attempt new, more effective strategies on the job and in their personal lives.

We want to believe

we are 'right'

We think we have to

be 'right' in

order to be loved.

© Copyright Lynn Ellsworth Taylor, November 1997

6

Why We Always Hurt the Ones We Love

Since our personality styles and the resulting strategies are created by our genetic pre-disposition, combined with our family of origin environment, we tend to subconsciously create adult situations within which we can continue to fight the same fights and get the same results we did while learning to survive through childhood and adolescence.

There are two predominant reasons why we do this. The first is ego driven. We want to believe that we are "right." We have a need to prove that the way we are, that the way we act, is correct. We believe that being right is the best way to get love, respect, attention and rewards. So, we continuously recreate the old dramas because the fact of our survival proves that our strategies have been right in the past and continue to be right in the present. We are terrified to change.

The second reason for staying true to our survival strategies (personal dramas) is the exact opposite of the first; It is a subconscious drive (spiritual pull). One of the primary forces in human existence is the desire for personal evolution, the desire to constantly improve, to figure life out and make some sense out of it. To achieve some level of self-fulfillment.

We, therefore, continue to recreate our childhood and adolescent dramas until we are able to discern that some of our strategies were not all that productive and successful. We cause ourselves the same frustrations and pains over and over again, finding ways to recreate family of origin conflicts in our adult homes and in the work-place until we finally create enough pain and frustration in ourselves that we are willing to look at the truth about our ineffectiveness and decide that the risk of trying something else is less threatening than the continuation of our ineffective patterns. By this means we pull ourselves by the boot straps up through personal evolution.

For both of these reasons we tend to "hurt the ones we love"— the ones we work with and with whom we have created our most important relationships.

The purpose of this discussion is not to encourage Professional Personality Index testing and the following discussions to be group therapy workshops, but to provide a simple understanding of human nature to each participant so the learning which is facilitated by this process will have its maximum impact on all involved. Each participant must find his or her own way to utilize the new personal information that is derived from this process.

I believe, if provided a good understanding of the simple description of our life process in this chapter, people will be more inclined to accept the new insights which are being offered by the test results and by feedback from others— will be more inclined to take on the challenges which necessarily follow: More direct conflict with others, more clear boundaries and work expectations, more visibility regarding performance. These things can be very threatening, but if seen as a necessary requirement for the job and for personal development, the perceived value of proceeding and participating fully will be significantly enhanced.

7

How Can They Think Like That?
Our Spiritual Cornerstones.

Have you ever left a meeting with a herd of engineers, or a flock of marketing and sales people, saying to yourself, "How can they think like that?" Or, after having a fight with your boss, made the statement to the first person you met, "I just don't get where she's coming from." All of us at times look at the people around us, amazed at the strangeness of their point of view.

And that's just what it is, a different point of view. Each personality style has a different perspective on the world. Each perspective has its basis in a deep-seated spiritual dispensation, a propensity to rely on one spiritual value more than any other. This core value is like the cornerstone of a building, all other stones of thought, action and attitude are aligned with it and built upon it.

When this alignment is made consciously, with knowledge of the cornerstone value and its desired effects, a person's life becomes beneficial, effective and fulfilling. When this alignment is done in the dark of emotional disorder, fear, anger at the past, unresolved grief, lust or greed, the stones which are aligned to the cornerstone are false stones and the alignment is crooked, demanding extreme rationalization.

PRIMARY SPIRITUAL VALUES
BANKER

Knowledge

Justice

© Copyright Lynn Ellsworth Taylor, November 1997

The degree to which this misalignment exists in each of us is the degree to which our most powerful characteristics and chosen traits become our weaknesses.

This misalignment of personality strategies with a person's cornerstone value creates a false wall which separates people; It positions one personality against another, and excites enmity. It is this type of personality block which I have found to be a major factor in the frustrations of business managers with their teams. This kind of personality weakness shows up time and again as a primary reason that a department or business performance is operating at substandard levels.

The Spiritual Cornerstone of Bankers

The spiritual cornerstone of a Banker is knowledge, knowledge in all its forms and functions. Knowledge is the basis for all human progress, both in society and in each individual. From the first attempts of a child to speak, through the personal evolution of each individual toward self-awareness, to the last thoughts of a great thinker expressed to guide humanity in its next steps, knowledge is the primary ingredient which makes everything possible.

Knowledge is the basis of all business, all political systems, all social organizations. Science, music, religion, literature, commerce; All human enterprises begin and end with knowledge.

A painter knows how to mix colors and how to build the illusion of three dimensions into a two dimensional painting. A bricklayer understands the mixing of mortar and the cutting and setting of bricks. A scientist knows the mathematics and the chemical make-up of things, allowing experimentation to lead to innovation.

Business people who set for themselves the task of building commercially successful operations have to have basic knowledge in finance, manufacturing, accounting, marketing, sales, management of people. Underlying these obvious knowledge areas are the fundamentals of algebra, psychology, physics, electronics, economics, reading, writing and arithmetic. Without appropriate knowledge in each of these areas businesses fail.

A Banker who allows the primary value of knowledge to lead him into pursuit of greater knowledge, into sincere application of existing information, is an invaluable resource. The Banker mind desires complete knowledge, detailed information, utilitarian facts and data. And, since the only purpose of knowledge is to educate and guide others in their enterprises (practical application), a powerful Banker is committed to and excels in the ability to present and disseminate his knowledge which is gathered and analyzed so carefully.

In order to be a fully developed Banker there must be a commitment to acquisition of knowledge about one's self. A Banker who makes this knowledge first in priority is driven not by a desire to control others through development of expertise and specific knowledge, but rather by the profound spiritual desire to open minds, guide thoughts and bring more practical application of knowledge into the work place, into the world.

PRIMARY SPIRITUAL VALUES
INNOVATOR

Wisdom

Compassion

© Copyright Lynn Ellsworth Taylor, November 1997

Bankers who are stuck in their need for controlling others, who are fearful of losing their indispensability, withhold information. They give incomplete instructions and answer essay questions with yes or no, true or false answers. Some Bankers are very successful in their effort to make the world around them march to their peculiar Banker drum.

I have seen Bankers take whole companies down by secreting their information, making themselves feared tyrants or seemingly indispensable workers, making of simple tasks an amazingly complex labyrinth of undocumented procedures and hidden sources of essential information. Computers with passwords and encrypted files with hieroglyphics for titles (C:\wp51\accou\pln.spd) all serve the power hungry Banker's urge for control.

"Here, let me do that. You'll just mess it up." "What are you going to do while I'm gone? No one else around here cares about any of this stuff."

Love of knowledge is just as insidious as the love of money or power and often a lot harder to identify. A Banker who is feeling pushed or who is working in a threatening environment will often use his knowledge to undermine, resist, deflate, over-ride, cause delay and just generally control the work place with it. If unsuccessful at controlling his environment with his knowledge, he will attempt to control the people around him by volunteering to "...do a little research on this. I'll get back to you," thereby keeping everyone waiting expectantly for the Banker's perfect conclusion on the subject.

The secondary spiritual value for Bankers is Justice. They have a drive to see that their knowledge is fairly applied to all people and all situations including themselves. This sense of justice when directed outwardly toward society is what makes Bankers take action, it makes them want to share their knowledge with the world, freely, openly. It is very difficult even for very mature Bankers to continue sharing their knowledge when they feel they are unjustly treated or when they see their knowledge being misused by others for unjust causes.

Important. The self esteem of a Banker personality is founded in the sense of worth, the value of his or her personal knowledge and expertise. The only thing that makes a Banker act out in negative ways is the reality or the Banker's belief that her Knowledge is not valued or is not being appropriately applied. When a Banker's Knowledge is not treated justly a Banker suspends the personal requirement to seek justice for others.

The Spiritual Cornerstone of Innovators

Wisdom is the spiritual cornerstone upon which Innovators build. Wisdom is the profound and essential attribute which allows a person or a society to make choices. Wisdom is the ability to discern options and to weigh one option over another through extrapolation of consequences and projection of likely results.

Wisdom is applied knowledge, basic facts turned into understanding, perceived truth. The Innovator's decision to base her life on the pursuit and perfection of Wisdom is a smart choice. Banker's may develop millions of megabytes of data and esoteric information, but it is the Innovator's capacity for quick and thorough assessment, prioritization, reconfiguration, taking another look from another aspect— this Innovator Wisdom unlocks the power of the Banker's knowledge and sets it to work.

The wisdom of Innovators keeps company presidents from throwing the baby out with the bath water. It makes the conception and design of products possible. It opens market opportunities and resolves conflicts with vendors, customers and employees. Wisdom is the linchpin of all problem-solving. Wisdom applied in the work place makes on-going success a realizable dream. It makes downturns in the economy just another problem to solve. No set of circumstances will defeat the wisdom of an Innovator who is not caught up in personality dramas or feeling fearful.

When backed into a corner, however, the Wisdom of an Innovator becomes cleverness, deceitfulness, distraction. An Innovator is perfectly willing to use her wisdom to present two arguments with equal weight, to throw whole groups of unsuspecting business people into indecision, either through clever argumentation or through presentation of complex facts and ideas which are not resolvable at face value.

Innovators love to show their ingenuity, especially when others appear to be floundering. So Innovators who are seeking control of a situation will cause chaotic thought, will confuse the issues with unrelated facts or will simply change the subject. More likely an Innovator will add one more layer of complexity each time someone else appears to be heading toward a decision. This keeps the focus of the group on the Innovator and gives the Innovator the chance to be the heroic problem-solver.

The wisdom of an Innovator who is seeking control creates chaos, indecision, confusion and anger. An Innovator who feels the group moving against her favorite plan will throw additional disaster prophesies into the mix and then suggest a regrouping later, during which delay the Innovator intimates that she will… "come up with an appropriate plan."

If the Innovator has established any respect for her previous solutions this tactic is highly successful. No one will act without hearing the wise counsel of the Innovator. And no one, no one can get the controlling Innovator to think faster, share her thoughts sooner or get a decision made before she is good and ready.

Once an Innovator has set such a course, subverting her Wisdom to clever leveraging and control, she is likely to use the resulting leverage to gain additional advantages over other people or to elevate her position in the organization. The wisdom of an Innovator misapplied can be a terribly disruptive force in the office or factory.

The secondary spiritual value of Innovators is compassion. Since Innovators are able to make quick assessments which lead to an understanding of people and situations they are able to empathize with others, understanding the why and the underlying motivations of others' actions. This makes Innovators very strong team players.

Important. The self esteem of an Innovator is almost entirely based upon the perception that his or her wisdom is valued by others, is being applied to worthy life situations and is perceived by others as wisdom. An Innovator personality does not resort to negative strategies unless this high valuation of personal Wisdom is truly threatened or perceived by the Innovator to be threatened. When an Innovator loses that sense of valued Wisdom they lose their compassion for themselves and others.

The Spiritual Cornerstone of Merchants

Merchants hang their hats on Love. What a holy place to hang a hat. I begin with Merchants this way for two reasons: One) because their holier-than-thou attitude can be repugnant, and Two) to keep Builders and Bankers from gagging during this discussion. Only Merchants will truly identify with love, not because they are the only loving people but because Merchants, more than any other personality type, value relationships and the required love that bonds relationships above all other factors in life.

Merchants look for opportunities to connect with other people. They desire openness and closeness with their fellow workers. They put themselves out for others and take social and emotional risks to build good relationships. Love is the highest form of abstraction, requiring perception, aesthetic appreciation, awe in the presence of beauty. Love is the glue that holds people together when everything else deserts them.

Merchants are the artists, musicians and actors in this world. They give themselves totally to their assignments and generate passion, excitement and enthusiasm because of this. It is the desire to give and receive love which drives them and makes them irresistible forces.

Merchants will present themselves as peacemakers, entertainers, therapists, good friends, quiet listeners, excited sales agents—whatever role is necessary to help build bridges, decrease conflict and improve the nature of relationships— in short to generate love.

But Merchants, when backed against the wall, or when they feel their trust has been broken, will cut others off. And once a Merchant's patient and forgiving attitude has been breached (in their opinion) they become the most unforgiving of the lot. They have made themselves more vulnerable, more available, more accepting than other personality types and expect themselves to be treated appropriately. When they do not feel reciprocity they turn to the far side of love.

The far side looks like this. First, you may hear a complaint about the poor treatment. Next will come the accusation of wrong-doing, followed shortly by the judgment that the person in question is "not good." Manipulation, acting pleasant in order to appear superior and above the fray, garnering support from others, black-balling the offending co-worker— these are the tools put to work by the "loving" merchant when he wants to control the situation, when he wants to re-establish his sense of being loved and protect himself from further hurt.

Merchants not only want to control what happens but also the manner, the style, the feelings around what happens. They want to set the tone, control the pace, have their fingers in the whole pie. Builders and Bankers are very wary of the Merchant because the idea of founding anything on something as intangible as love is strange to them in the first place. Second, they have trouble

PRIMARY SPIRITUAL VALUES
MERCHANT

Love

Truth

© Copyright Lynn Ellsworth Taylor, November 1997

discerning real love from the manipulation of overly exuberant Merchants. So it is better to distrust and push off these "too soft and fuzzy" Merchants, keep them at a distance where they can be watched and not cause too much harm.

The cornerstone of love adopted by the Merchant as the highest value, when darkened by the need to control others, becomes a very deceptive and mean tool of manipulation and malice. Beware the Merchant who has decided you are "not very nice."

The secondary spiritual value of Merchants is Truth. Merchants secretly, intuitively know that without Truth, without a clear view of what is real, there is no love. If a person pretends to be what they are not, then any love which may come to that person is not intended for the real person but for the impersonator. This knowledge leaves a Merchant always looking for the actual Truth of situations, especially regarding one's self.

Important. The self esteem of a Merchant is almost entirely based in his or her sense of being loved, being perceived as a loving person, the perception of self as a loving person. Merchants do not resort to negative strategies unless this Love perception is threatened, whether the threat is real or imagined. When a Merchant feels unloved the commitment to Truth is rationalized away. Unconsciously the Merchant strategy decides that any means required to regain the sense of being loved is okay.

The Spiritual Cornerstone of Builders

The cornerstone of a Builder is Power; The power of action, work, energy, physical labor, tangible results, commands, decisiveness, bricks and mortar and roaring machines. Builders love chain saws and bulldozers and in the business community tend to be chain saws and bulldozers.

But the power of Builders is clear and spiritual. They are the purity of straight forward speech, bottom line thinking, calling B.S., looking for a simple approach, stepping ahead, accepting risk, leading others into action. The power of a Builder inspires action in others, gives others a sense of well-being, confidence.

When a Builder is benevolent, on task, purposeful and charged with a short term mission, her work has the strength of right and irresistibility behind it. Builders have a good feeling at the end of the day if they are tired, hungry and horny. This natural, strong, uncorrupted presence is a delight for those who appreciate the smell of mown hay, the fresh dust from saws at a building sight, the color black on corporate profit charts.

If a Builder feels confused she will take an action, trusting that the action will create a new situation, and that in the new situation she will be able to quickly decide upon another appropriate action. Builders are more driven by faith than any other personality type. They have confidence in their own power and trust the basic right of their gut instincts.

When Builders are directly challenged, they tend to immediately engage their power in battle for dominance. If dominance is not easily gained, they elevate their power to a higher level, seeking to intimidate those who resist them.

PRIMARY SPIRITUAL VALUES
BUILDER

Power

Faith

© Copyright Lynn Ellsworth Taylor, November 1997

Since a Builder's actions are based on gut instinct and supported by a faith in their own power, they cannot allow themselves to be seen as being wrong. This possibility in the Builder's mind of taking wrong action undermines her cornerstone of power, making the cornerstone wrong. This is "not acceptable," (a term you will often hear from Builders).

In order to maintain the position of being right, a Builder will interrupt, bluster, threaten, intimidate, physically rise above you, rage, charge through open spaces and invade any one's space who dares defy her. She expects immediate and absolute compliance and capitulation. These expectations and the accompanying actions often give the Builder the illusion of power which she is seeking in order to feel in control.

Once the illusion of control is re-established, the Builder will immediately return to hard work, not recognizing or understanding that harm may have been done to another person, that a relationship may have been destroyed temporarily if not permanently.

Power, when misapplied by the Builder to gain and keep control over others, becomes a sledge hammer applied to a finishing nail. It may drive the nail home, but it ruins the walls of the house it is meant to help build. Since power appears to have an absolute quality Builders also tend to be independent and unwilling to rely on others. Their foundation in power, if not balanced by the other cornerstones of knowledge, love and wisdom, will yield business results for a time, but the experience of success will be spoiled by the absence of a team to share the glory. The Builder will find herself like the band leader with no band to lead.

Important. A Builder's self esteem is mostly dependent upon his or her sense of personal appropriate power. Only when a Builder feels powerless, not allowed to act or has the perception that personal power is not currently being valued or applied to worthy tasks- only then will the Builder resort to negative strategies. Builders are just as vulnerable as every other personality style that's why they hate so much to admit it— their vulnerability feels like the opposite of power and makes them extremely nervous— fearful.

Building a Business with Four Corners

Every business requires all four cornerstones to be in place in order to assure success. When the primary value of any one personality type is allowed to control, the strength of that personality style becomes the weakness that brings the house down.

As a business grows the value that is needed most during each phase is very different. At first it may be essential to value love, building relationships, attracting customers, serving them with unfailing attention. As more customers are attracted the attributes of work and power become more required in order to meet commitments.

Soon the complexities of the business created by its success begin to overwhelm all of the players, and the need for wisdom, problem-solving, new systems and better plans begins to take precedence. Conservation, better knowledge of the competition, superior technical skills, better handling of financial concerns— these elements of knowledge become the most essential cornerstone— until the risk aversion of the Bankers begins to stall the company and flatten its growth, once again elevating the Merchant's commitment to opportunity and relationships to the highest plain.

How We Each Build Our Self Esteem

Since each personality style comes into a business with a totally different view of the world, a different sense of values, they tend to see each other as enemies, or obstacles, or nuisances. It is the search for a strong self esteem which drives us all.

The **Banker** derives self-esteem from the quality of and apparent need for her knowledge, and her strong sense of justice is kept in good order as long as this feeling of esteem is in place. But when a situation becomes too risky, or people seem to not value her knowledge, the Banker's esteem is deflated, and the sense of justice magically disappears and is replaced by a harsh judgment of others. The world, after all, is not valuing the knowledge offered so there is no longer any justice in the world.

Once a Banker perceives an absence of justice around her, all bets are off. The Banker is willing to withdraw all participation from whatever game is being played. This usually does not mean physically leaving. There is simply a complete lack of action or effort. The Banker expends no energy when her esteem is at stake. The Builder may be raging, the Merchant manipulating and exaggerating, the Innovator throwing confusion into the system, all to regain control.

But the Banker's strategy is masterful. Wait. Refuse to play. Outlast everyone. The Banker settles back into a reservoir of knowledge and waits for opportunity to arise. As the Builder's impatience rises, the Banker adds fuel to the fire. This leaves the Merchant feeling vulnerable in the face of serious conflict, setting him into the exposed

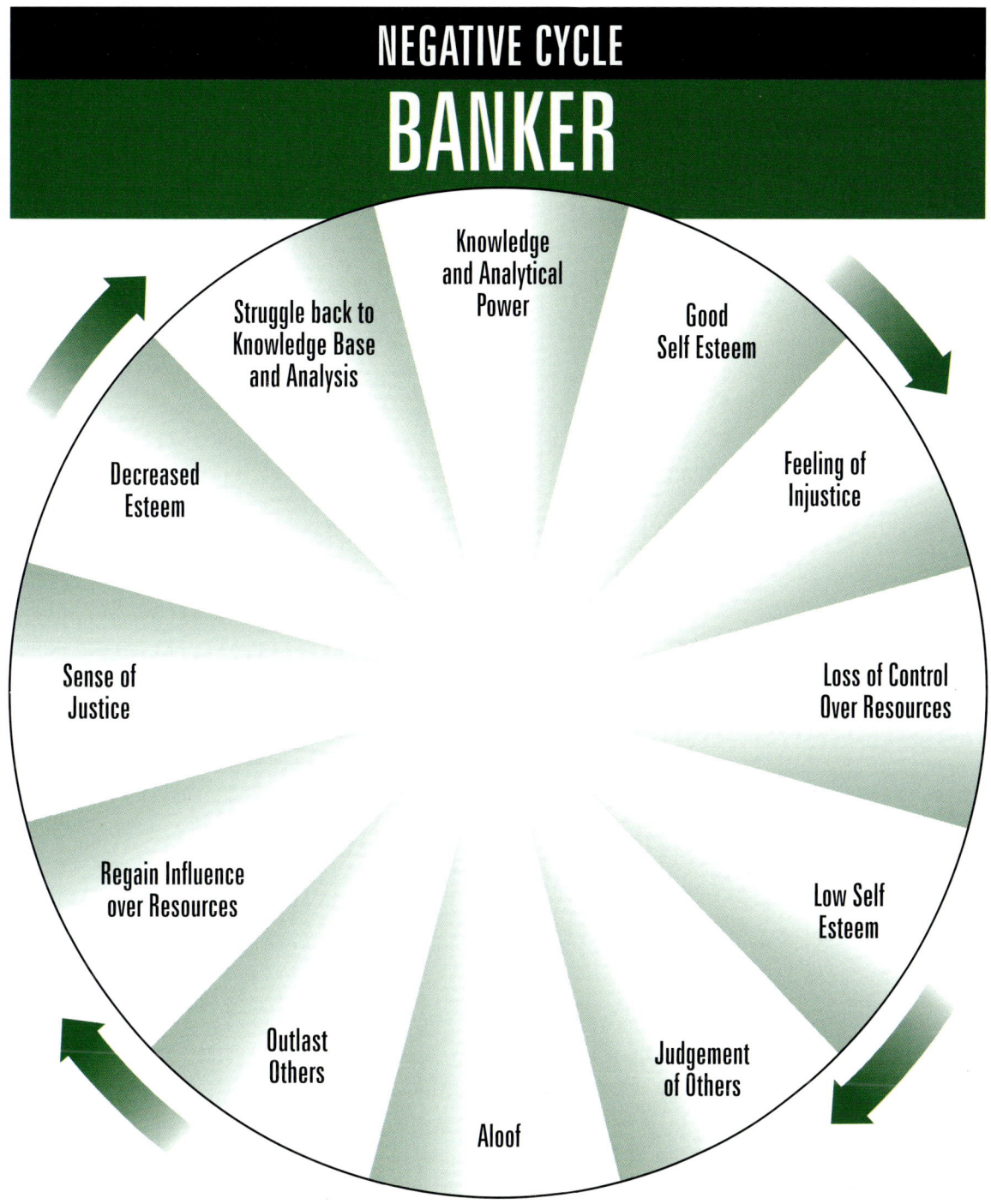

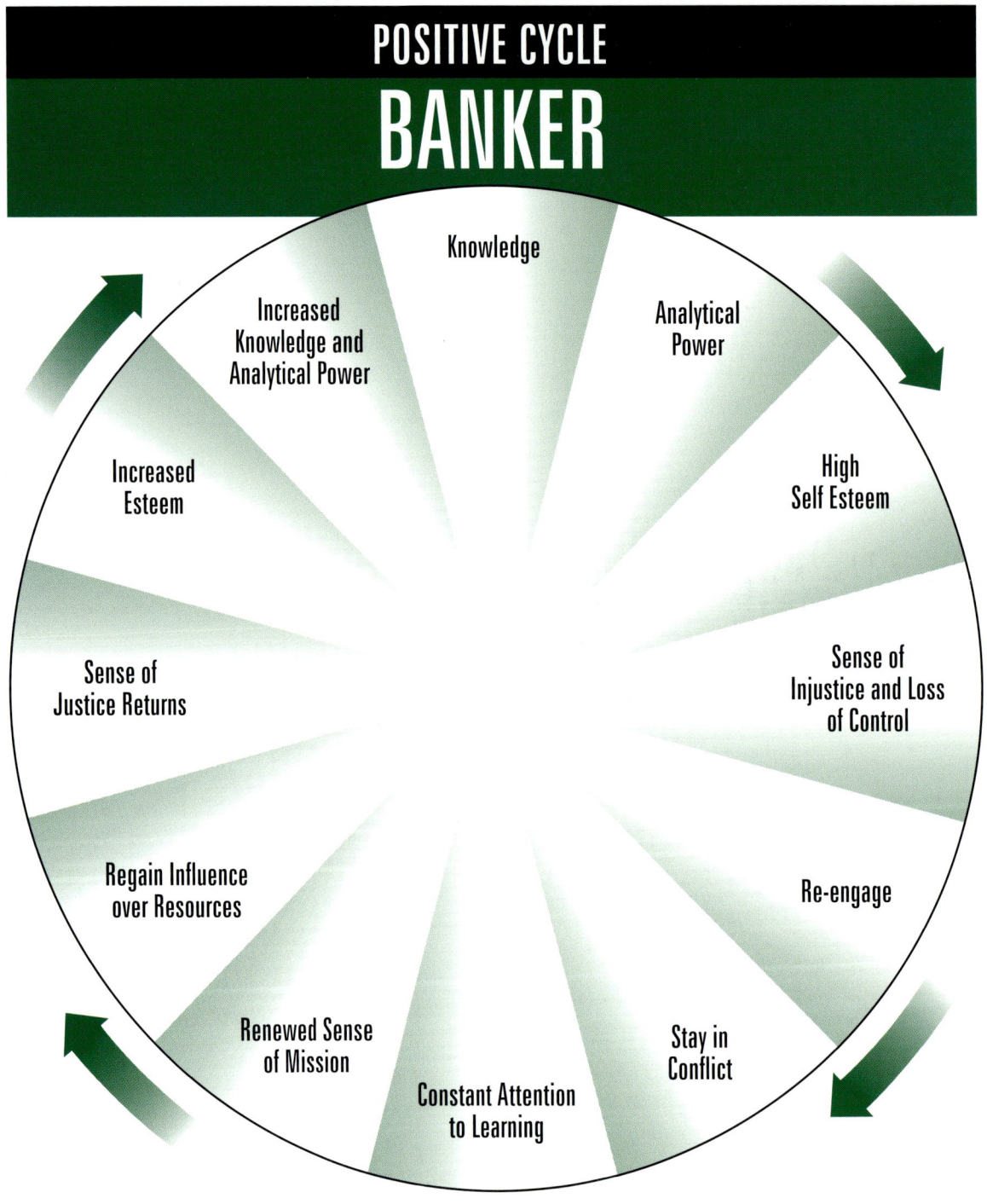

position of exaggerating present opportunities, which the Banker is able to shoot down with facts concerning past failures.

And when the Innovator kicks in a clear and reasonable solution to the business problem, the Banker is ready with an arsenal of challenging propositions all of which lead to disaster, fomenting an intolerably complex problem. Then when everyone turns their excited, angry energy in the direction of the Banker out of fear, anger and frustration, the Banker pulls out the ultimate weapon. She becomes aloof.

The aloof Banker cannot be intimidated, cannot be manipulated or cajoled, cannot be interrogated or cross examined. An aloof Banker in leadership regains control by outlasting all the others, and refusing to join in the ruckus. When all the others are panting and out of breath, the Banker claims the right of survivor and exerts the basic position of knowledge, a lot like playing the Ace of Spades into a royal flush on the last hand.

The mature Banker, remains true to her own sense of justice and relies upon the founding quality of real expertise, real knowledge to eventually rule. And, having applied her thirst for knowledge first to self-awareness, the mature Banker is quick to recover from an attack of aloofness.

The Banker's self-esteem is founded in Knowledge, and measured by a sense of justice. No amount of power, wisdom or love can provide the Banker with self-esteem. To attempt to do so is a waste of life.

Merchants derive self-esteem from the quality of love around them, from the apparent need of others for their Merchant love. As long as this seems real, then Truth is the Merchant's balancing value. Merchants are more willing to explore Truth at more levels in more areas of concern than any other personality style: Personal, family, work, society, religion.

However, when a Merchant feels unloved and unappreciated, or when he feels his trust has been broken, a Merchant turns from a seeker of truth to a purveyor of lies. He will exaggerate in order to appear more important, dramatize in order to gain attention, lie in order to cover up for incomplete work. When a Merchant forgets to love himself and to remain steady in the face of criticism he loses all sense of esteem. "Love is missing. How can I get it back?"

Since the Merchant is more likely to accept others, he is often found to be gullible, trusting too much, not holding on to skepticism as tightly as might be reasonable. So the Merchant feels set up, deceived. This entitles the Merchant to withdraw love from the offending person or group, sacrificing his own commitment to truth and deserting his requirement to be involved constantly with love.

The Merchant goes into a frenzy at this point, trying to perform, trying to manipulate, to cajole, to win everyone over. There is even a residual need to win over the person or persons who have offended him. These tactics are sometimes effective, which encourages the Merchant to continue using these tactics. If the tactics are not effective the Merchant pouts and denies the personal value of the offenders.

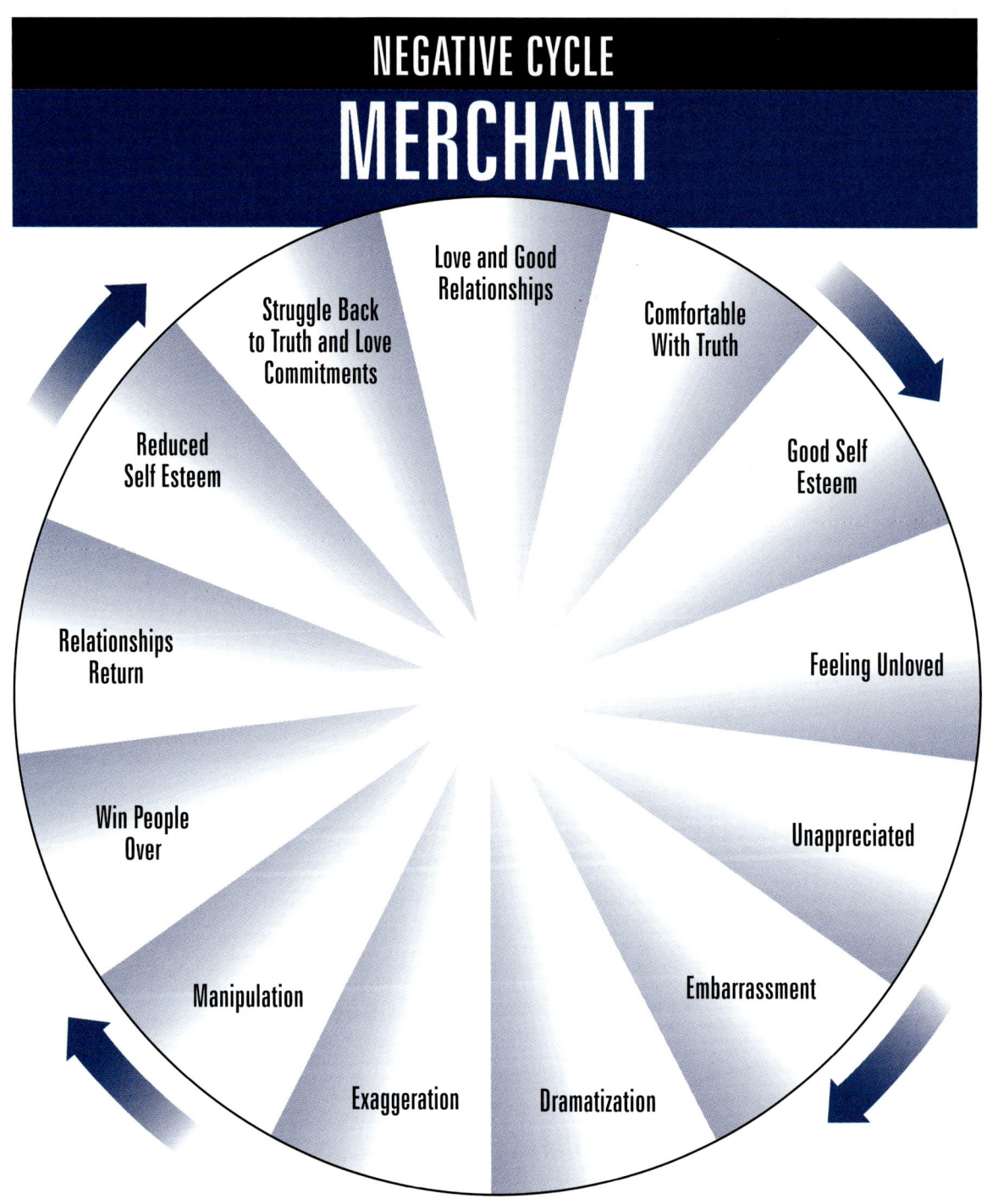

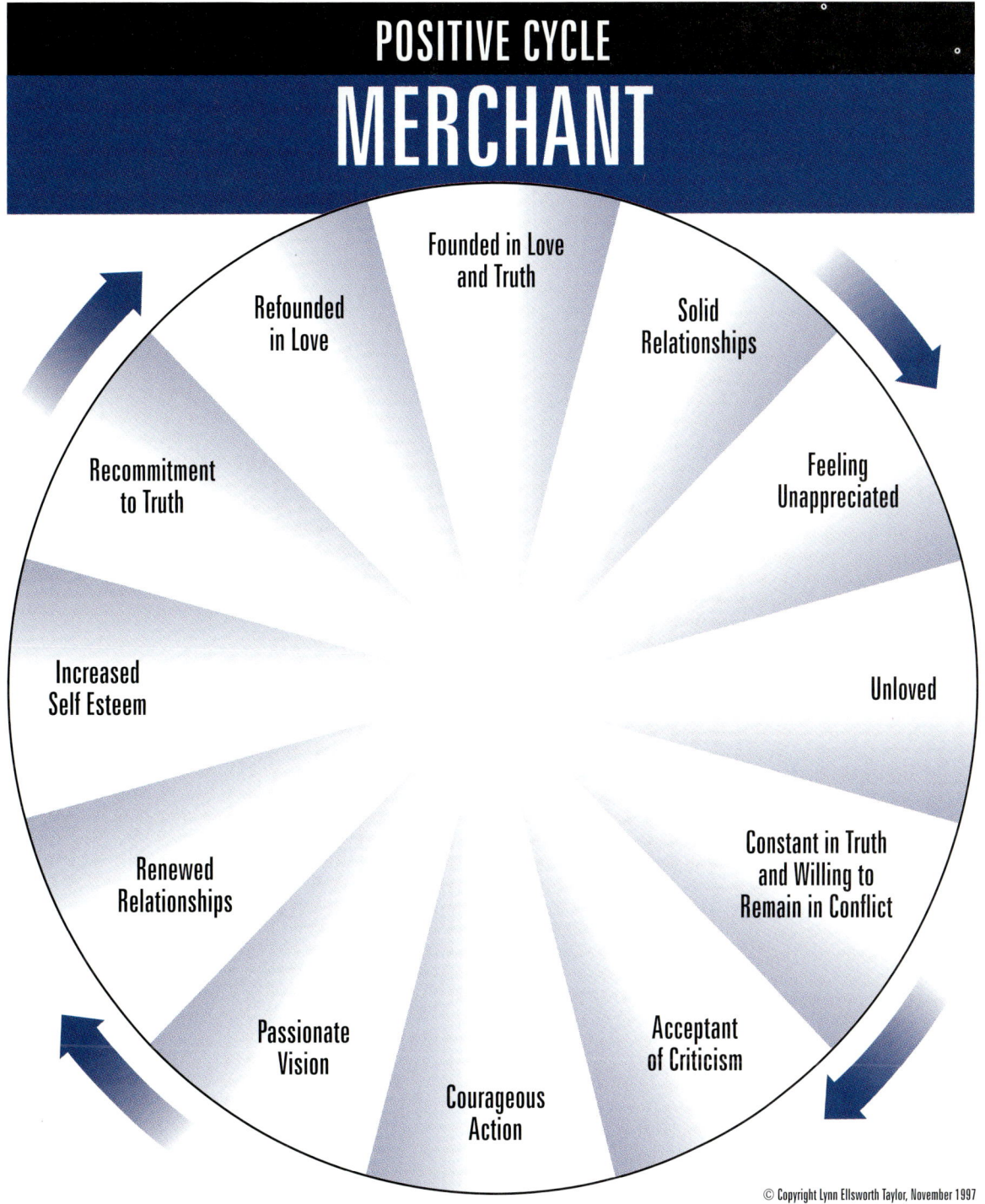

The mature Merchant, however, remains open and committed to his relationships, is willing to stay engaged in conflict and trusts that good will come of it. His commitment to truth keeps him from falling back into exaggeration (lying) and allows him to accept whatever responsibility is his for an undesired result. This steadiness and consistency in relationship with others makes lasting friends of those around him and builds trust. The power of the mature Merchant grows exponentially during serious difficulties.

The **Innovator** derives self-esteem from the complexity of the problems against which she is matched. The bigger the problem, the more robust and valued the Innovator feels. When this feeling of esteem is fully in bloom the Innovator's Wisdom is balanced by a second spiritual quality, Compassion (Understanding).

An Innovator who is acting out of strong self-esteem is perceptive and open to all kinds of influence. She becomes tolerant, accepting and forgiving, able to see people and situations clearly, without judgment. This allows an Innovator to be compassionate, rising to a higher level of thinking than the other personality types who are more likely to become caught up in the fray, especially Merchants and Builders. The mature Innovator understands how others might be caught up in ineffective behavior and seeks to find ways to bring the team back together.

However, when the Innovator feels controlled and pushed, required to settle on a solution too rapidly or when others appear to dismiss her best ideas casually and without understanding the full intent, the Innovator is merciless.

This is the negative cycle of an immature Innovator. She moves from wisdom and compassion into accusation, from compassion into interrogation, from wisdom into cleverness and sabotage. As she matures, however, she learns to remain patient, to listen and observe until clear solutions come. She learns not to fall back into interrogation, attempting to throw others off. She remains committed to acknowledging her own ignorance and to looking for the opportunity to gain more understanding.

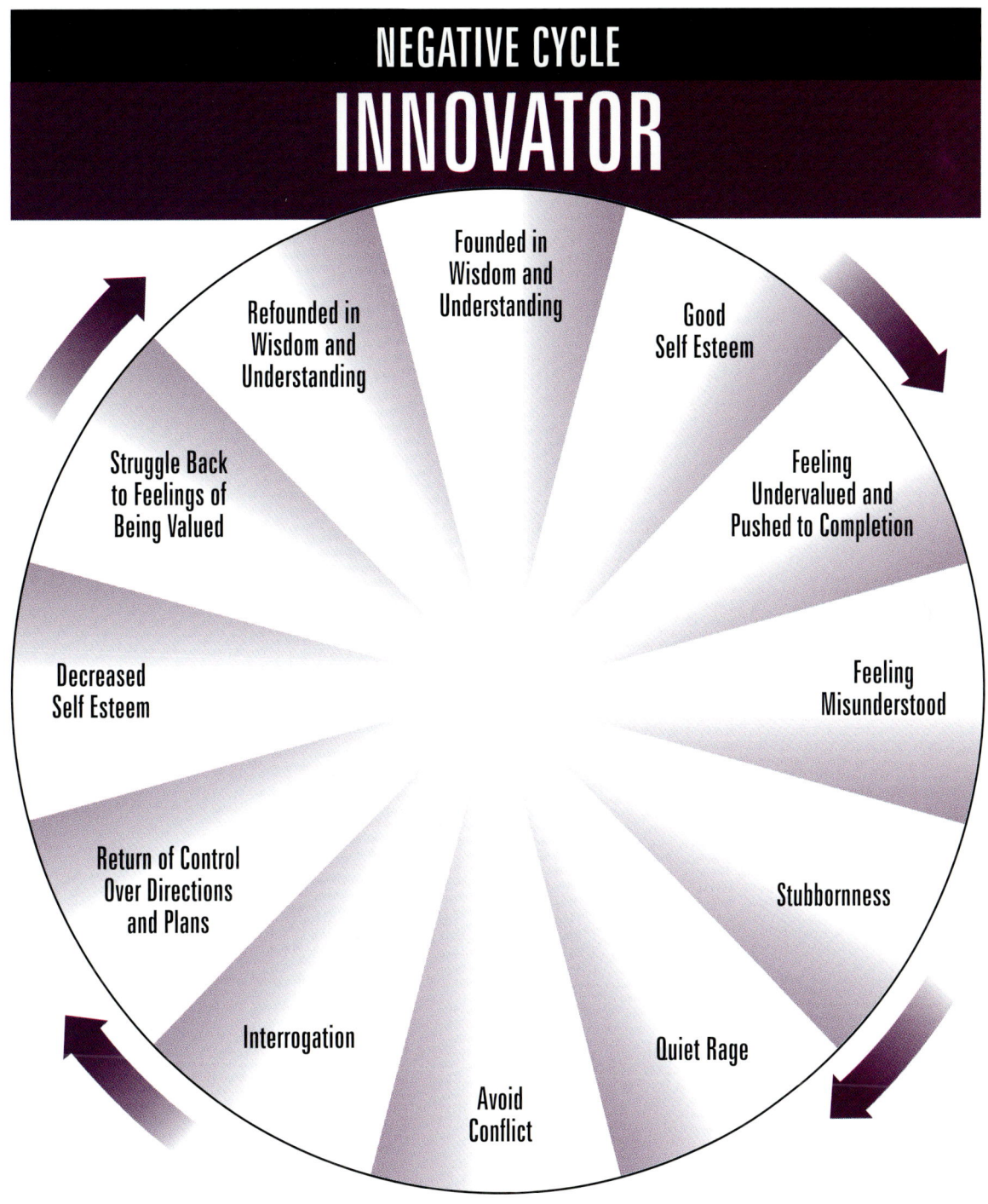

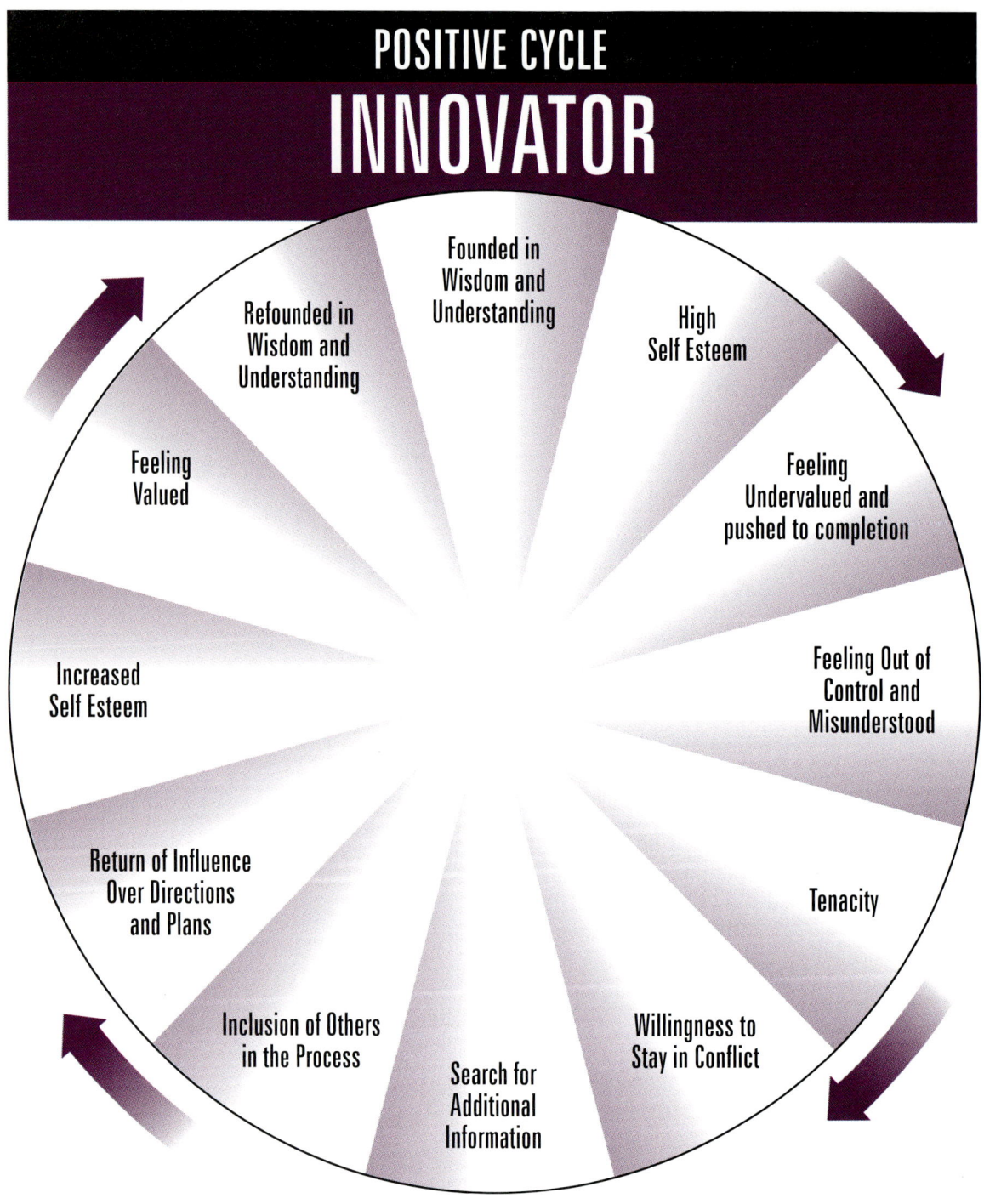

The mature Innovator applies her wisdom to present troubles and looks for solutions to present conflicts, becoming the reasonable voice in a harried crowd. By sitting back and watching the Innovator is able to see others as they really are and to maintain an attitude of understanding and acceptance. This stance makes the mature Innovator a respected counselor and a valued advocate in difficult situations.

The **Builder's** self esteem is founded in the tangible evidence of applied personal power. Her secondary spiritual quality is Faith. There is a faith in the basic goodness of others, faith in the goodness of action, of striving to create, of being productive. The Builder acts because she believes that by acting she will be guaranteed a reward. The Builder does not look for justice or mercy, only effectiveness and results. Every action must receive an equivalent reward.

So the Builder is more able to continue to act because of her reliance on faith. When her faith is lost, when rewards do not equal effort, when the balance is thrown against the Builder, all sense of power is lost. She becomes impotent. Self-esteem is lost. All reliance upon Power is proven ineffective. The world is no longer fair. This brings out the intimidator.

If there is no balance, no reward for expended power then other means are justified. If people are not being good, acting within the confines of the Builder's faith system, then an opposite action is required, intimidation. The opposite of faith is the taking of absolute control, the willingness to kill or be killed.

The Builder goes into battle willing to risk everything in order to regain control, in order to be able to take positive action again. Once this natural order is re-established the Builder can once again rely on her faith. This is the power/faith, impotence, intimidation, faith/power cycle of an immature Builder.

The mature Builder, however, becomes an almost irresistible force, since her faith remains constant, encouraging continued positive action, until her faith is at last proven right. This increases the Builder's willingness to exert powerful action even in the face of risk and failure. I never want to be in a business situation without one clear-minded, powerful, faith-filled builder working on my team.

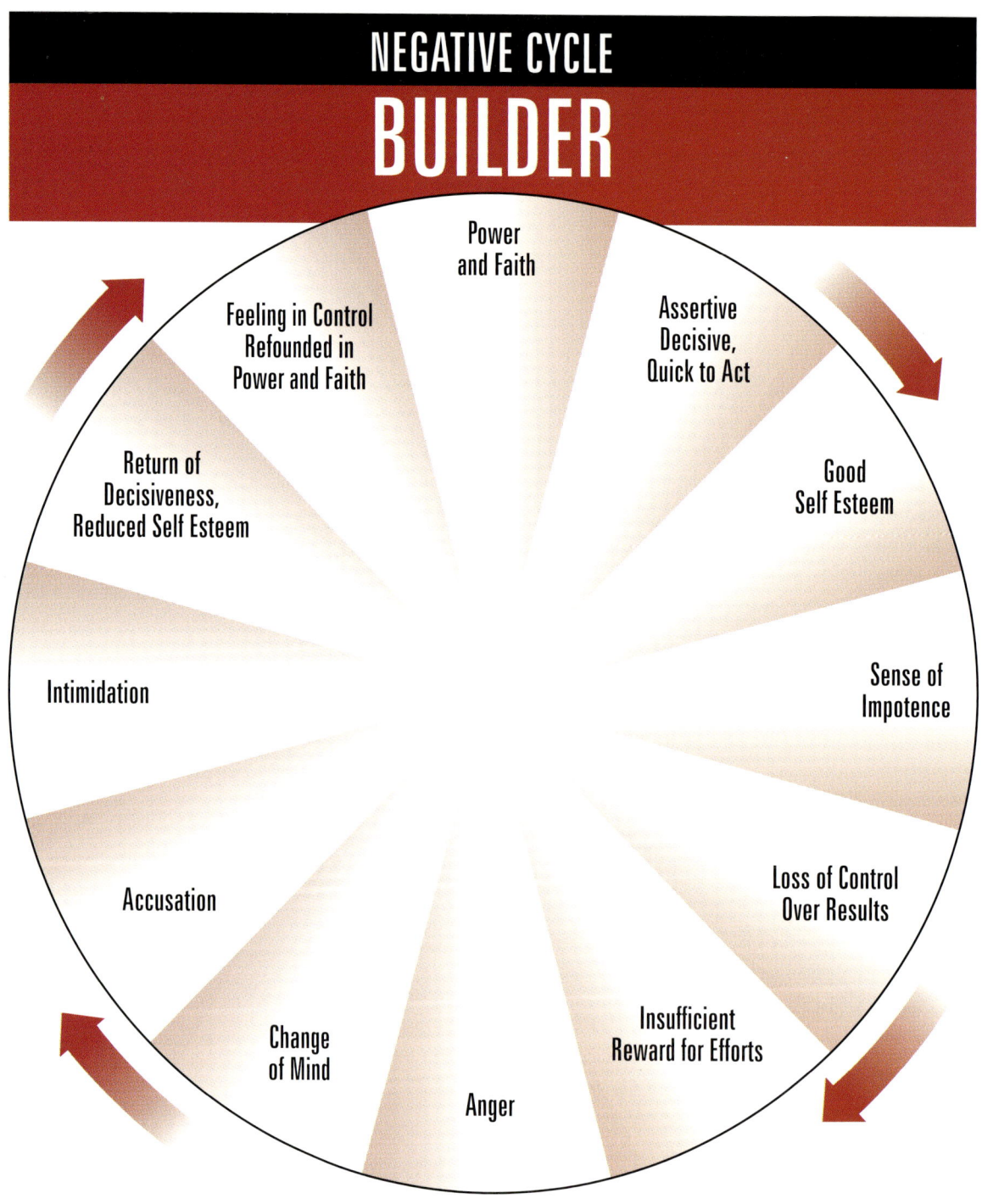

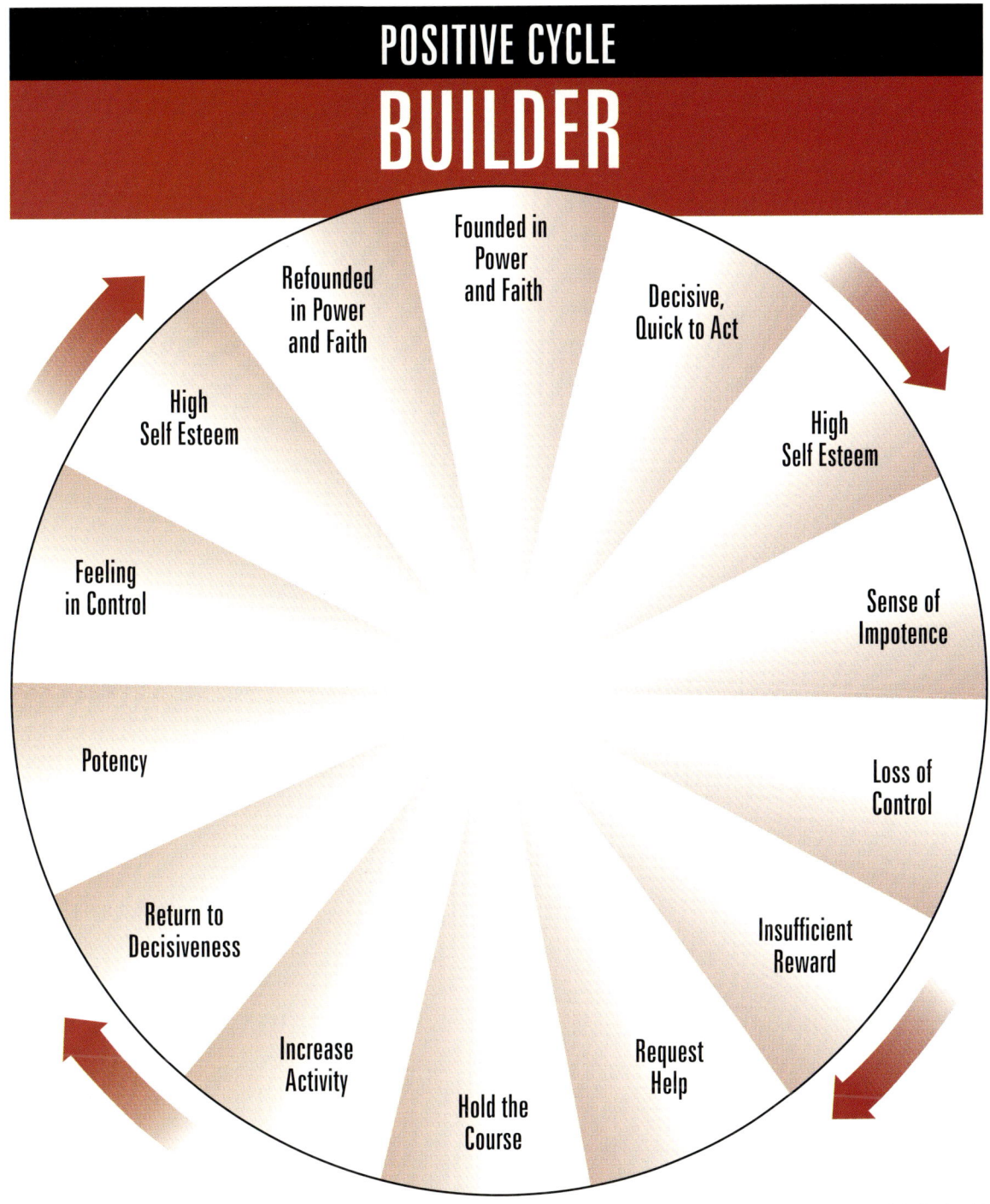

What I

don't know

about myself

controls my life

© Copyright Lynn Ellsworth Taylor, November 1997

8

How Can I Change Who I am?

What we really mean when we ask this question, is, "How can I change my behavior? or How can I increase my success?— How can I keep my foot out of my mouth? or Where do I find the courage to take more risks— to be more outgoing?" We all want to be our best self, to accomplish our dreams, to feel that our lives have meaning. But the ways we have learned to react to different situations and to different people often spoil our sense of a good self.

So, the secret is to give up the idea of changing yourself and take possession of your life. Claim the powerful, loving, creative and knowledgeable elements of your life and build on them. Instead of trying to change who you are habitually being, the challenge is to find your way back to being who you really are.

Each personality style without fear has a wonderful capable strategy for developing fulfillment and success in life. The idea is to reclaim your life from the edicts of parents, teachers and early social influences— to see yourself as the Banker-Innovator or other personality style that you are and to develop all of the positive aspects of your personality strategies, minimizing the negative reactions.

A young sales representative came to my office, frustrated with himself, with his company and with his boss whom he felt was competing with him. He was a strong Merchant-Builder who had spent his early career as an engineer and was now, at 33, learning the skills of selling, judging himself harshly and looking for reasons for his self imposed sense of failure. I did not judge him to be a failure. I was pleased with his progress after a few months of work with him and I told him so.

As Tom began his discourse on all of the reasons why he would not be able to succeed in the company where he was now working, I asked if we could start instead by talking about his personality style and whether he was helping or hurting himself. Okay.

While I was describing the strengths and weaknesses of a Merchant-Builder, I caught Tom smiling self consciously, then laughing audibly. "That sounds like me, all right. I start out talking with customers, build a great rapport and at some point I get real uncomfortable that I'm wasting their time so I shift instantly from being a Merchant to being a Builder and get down to business. Sometimes I can almost see them shrivel back away from me and the meeting ends with a cold feeling."

As we talked we learned that Tom's parents had both been harsh judges of him, getting impatient with him whenever he was too excited or when he wasn't talking about things they felt were important. That influence guided him toward engineering instead of sales. That influence still whispers in his ears today when he has "...taken enough of a customer's time chatting, and it's time to get down to business."

What I explained to Tom toward the end of this conversation applies to us all—

In Everyday Life,
Whatever Action We Take Because of Fear
is Wrong Action.

A confident, happy, robust person, regardless of the personality style, puts to work all of his positive personality traits intuitively, using skills and responses which have proven in the past to gain favor, win friends and influence enemies. Most of the time we as developing people act from this intuitive place. But when we experience ourselves being overpowered by someone, or unloved, or unappreciated, or judged as being wrong- we feel fearful. We get a tight knot in our stomachs. A voice in our head tells us to take defensive action and we react, shifting out of our positive self and into the negative traits of our personality styles.

Some of us shift from one personality trait to the next in order to escalate the conflict to a higher level and bring in the bigger guns of a different personality strategy. When we move from positive to negative or when we move from one personality strategy to another because of fear, we lose our effectiveness. We are no longer in control of ourselves or the situation. We can no longer take positive action since we are focused on deflecting the energy of someone else. We are on the defense.

Tom had found himself doing this very thing in a business meeting that same morning. He had been talking to his Sales Manager and to the company Controller, trying to understand as a group what had happened to a customer's invoice— how it had gotten screwed up. "I did all right," Tom said, "until they both started ganging up on me, and I knew they were wrong. Then, Suzy made me crazy by complaining that I hadn't given her the right information, and I lost it."

While telling me this story, Tom pointed his finger at a befuddled imaginative Suzy and told her off in no uncertain terms. Then he raised his hand in front of his face to show how his manager had backed him off and required him to settle down. He had left the meeting in a huff, with the issue unresolved, but having, in his own mind, won the argument, proven them both wrong and ready for the next assault.

I told Tom it sounded to me like he started the meeting as a compromising, listening Merchant and ended the meeting like a blustering Builder. He was willing to remain a Merchant, caring and responsive, until he felt unappreciated, overwhelmed and then made to feel wrong. At that point he feared being seen as incompetent, was afraid of being judged foolish, so he shifted to his Builder mode to take charge and force his point. He laid the blame powerfully in Suzy's lap and raised up his voice and his frame to make the impact felt.

It was the fear, I told him, that flipped the switch. And, when fear flips the switch the personality style called in for reinforcement is being called into battle with all negative strategies armed and ready. The same would be true if after leaving that meeting you had felt fearful of losing your job because of your anger and ineffectiveness at handling a small conflict. Your Merchant would have been called back in to fix the relationships, and you may have found yourself trying to manipulate Suzy and your boss back into liking you. They might have experienced you as being a little unctuous, a little too friendly and not trustworthy, especially considering your recent performance.

The trick is to be conscious of these switches which occur in all of us. One kind of incident will flip the fear switch sending a Builder in to rescue a Merchant. Another kind may send my personal Innovator in to interrogate some perceived enemy for my Banker side who is feeling judged. Regardless of the situation, when fear compels the action, the action comes out negatively.

As we become conscious of these switches which exist in each of us as a unique menu of responses, we can decide whether to respond out of fear or to remain engaged. We may still decide our best bet is to switch from one personality strategy to another, but when we do so it will be with the positive attributes of that personality style fully engaged. We will find ourselves acting more effectively, creating more relationship and business success because of this consciousness.

A strong Builder in Tom's situation above, could have been invited forward by Tom's Merchant as an assertive ally. This confident unafraid Builder might have repeated two or three times in an even voice, "Excuse me— Suzy, Suzy, excuse me. That's not how this happened. I gave you a memo yesterday. I can get it if you need me to, that clearly told you how this was to be billed, and how to communicate the decision to our customer. I will call the customer and straighten things out, but I need you to be more careful to follow that kind of instruction in the future."

Suzy would not have particularly like this response. In a way, although there would have been much less anger and hostility aroused in Tom, this powerful Builder response does not give Suzy any excuse to act out, to continue to argue, or to cut things off because Tom was being abusive. Tom would have left the meeting the clear-minded sales person who had done his job, with Suzy still needing to correct the situation and explain her own incompetence.

Tom's actual response had gotten Suzy off the hook, spoiled a few hours of happy selling and put one more black mark in his boss's mental notebook.

We are effective when we act without fear using the positive traits of the personality style we decide to employ at the moment.

As you become more skilled at recognizing the emotional and psychological switches that send you into the negative attributes of your primary or secondary personality styles, you will also gain a growing awareness of which personality styles are most effective in dealing with which situation and with which kind of person. You can become increasingly confident in the positive skills of all four personality styles, moving seamlessly from one to the other, always maintaining your sense of self control and personal power.

Watch and Learn

It is important as you begin this process to simply watch yourself responding to other people, in different challenging situations. Don't even attempt to correct your own action at this point. Just watch yourself going through your motions and notice how effective or ineffective you are being. And don't judge yourself harshly. After all, you were warped into this kind of stimulus response behavior over millions of years of evolution and a few decades of parental and social influence.

You have been doing the best you could. Now you're deciding to simply take a look at the relative effectiveness of your personality style choices and decide whether there might be a better way to act. The most important thing is to simply observe yourself in action. Tell yourself the truth about your own feelings. Know that all negative feelings are the result of fear. Ask yourself what you are afraid of that is making you react the way you are and listen to the answer.

Do this for several weeks, just watching and asking yourself to see the truth. At some point in the near future you will begin to understand the most devastating emotional switches to which you respond and you will be given the opportunity to think about a better strategy. When this begins to happen for you, come back to the Resource Guide and read through the personality style approaches. Ask yourself which personality style would be better at handling a given situation and commit yourself to move into that personality style the next time the fear comes up. Commit to act with all of the positive energy and resourcefulness of that chosen personality style. Commit yourself to watch, listen and learn whether this style works better for you in the observed situation. You will be amazed how dramatically this kind of conscious decision can change the outcome of challenging situations.

WHY WE CONFLICT

BUILDER
Power

Results

Short Term Action

MERCHANT
Love

Relationships

Long Term Vision

CONFLICT

BANKER
Analysis & Justice

Conservation

Knowledge

INNOVATOR
Solutions & Systems

Assessment

Wisdom

© Copyright Lynn Ellsworth Taylor, November 1997

9

Now that I know why I hate working with him, what do I do about it?

In the discussions that follow group testing using the Professional Personality Index, many latent and not so latent hostilities, frustrations and resentments may come to the surface. This is one of the powerful benefits of the Index. There is no need to be afraid of these arising conflicts.

My experience has been that the persons involved in surfacing the conflicts tend to grab the new information provided by the Index like shipwrecked survivors being thrown life vests from a passing ship. They know they have to put them on before the life vests can have any value and they know they still depend on others to help them get back on-board the ship.

Just the knowledge that much of the conflict is derived from persons who simply approach life in different ways provides a major shift of attitude. Merchants tend to quit seeing Builders as rude, arrogant, unfeeling S.O.B.'s and more as Builders who tend to resort to intimidating tactics when pressed or frustrated.

When the assumption of mean or negative motive is put aside and replaced with an understanding that the things I am experiencing (which I don't like) are simply survival tactics in the other person, much of the antipathy is removed from the situation. I can then see which tactics resound and clash with my own survival tactics and I can see that this interaction is exciting old personal dramas for me and possibly for others involved.

Builders still may find Merchants irritating but they will tend to have just a little more tolerance and may even decide that some forms of social niceties are not so disgusting as to be unacceptable business tactics, especially if a Builder wants to have a more successful and productive relationship with the Merchants in her life.

When we each shift in our awareness that the posture presented by other personality styles is not personal to us but is simply that person's chosen posture (strategy), we still may not invite them over for dinner, but we are given new tools (understandings) which will allow us to develop reasonably effective relationships with these people in a business setting. We will all waste a little less time bouncing off each other and more time focused on the business objectives at hand.

There are situations, however, where two or more people may have taken positions toward each other which are not surmountable with a few simple meetings. The individuals may not be able to go off together and reach a satisfactory resolution.

Often these strong oppositions and hostilities are encouraged by the management systems and business structures in the work place. One involved person may be the boss which makes for an uneven battle between individuals. Occasionally, one of the parties is unwilling to bend in any manner in their approach to the others, or is unwilling to forgive or trust the other(s) again.

When two or more people appear to be focused negatively on others with whom they must work on a regular basis, the following procedures for conflict resolution are recommended.

Conflict Resolution

One uninvolved person, preferably with good management, listening and negotiating skills will facilitate. The facilitator will state the ground rules and ask each person if they are willing to abide by the rules. Obtain an audible "yes" from each participant.

The Ground Rules

1. When one person is speaking, the other(s) will listen. Interrupting is not allowed no matter how "wrong," "inaccurate," "stupid," or "irritating," statements may be.

2. Each person will be given the opportunity to hear the other(s). Each person will be asked by the facilitator whether he or she has more to say, before going on to the next person.

3. The facilitator will take notes on the major points being expressed by each person. If a participant repeats a complaint, accusation or other point more than twice, the facilitator will acknowledge that the point has been covered and ask each other participant if they "heard" the point. Only "yes" or "no" answers are accepted here.

4. When each person has had a chance to speak, the facilitator will ask each to state their Dominant and Secondary Personality Index and to share the most ineffective strategy or tactic which results from their personality style. No feedback is allowed. Questions for clarity may be allowed as long as they are not leading and accusatory.

5. Once each has participated in this process, return to the list of concerns each has expressed. Reduce these concerns to a list of issues and ask the contributor of each list to agree that all major points have been covered.

6. Ask each other participant to acknowledge that they have heard the concerns and to state how and to what degree they feel they may be accountable for the on-going concern. No interruptions.

    Ask the question, "Is there anything else you might be willing to do to improve your relationship with "name?" Note: Do not allow anyone to refer to anyone else as "him or her." All comments must be directed to the individual and first names must be used.

7. Repeat steps six and seven until all parties have been heard and all concerns have been confronted.

8. List any concerns that appear to be unresolved. Adjourn the meeting with the requirement that each person involved in the unresolved disputes or concerns will think about appropriate business solutions to the conflict, and will also consider their own willingness to change their behavior to improve the effectiveness of their relationships. Ask for audible affirmation from each.

9. Reconvene a few days later and repeat steps 1-9, until all issues are resolved.

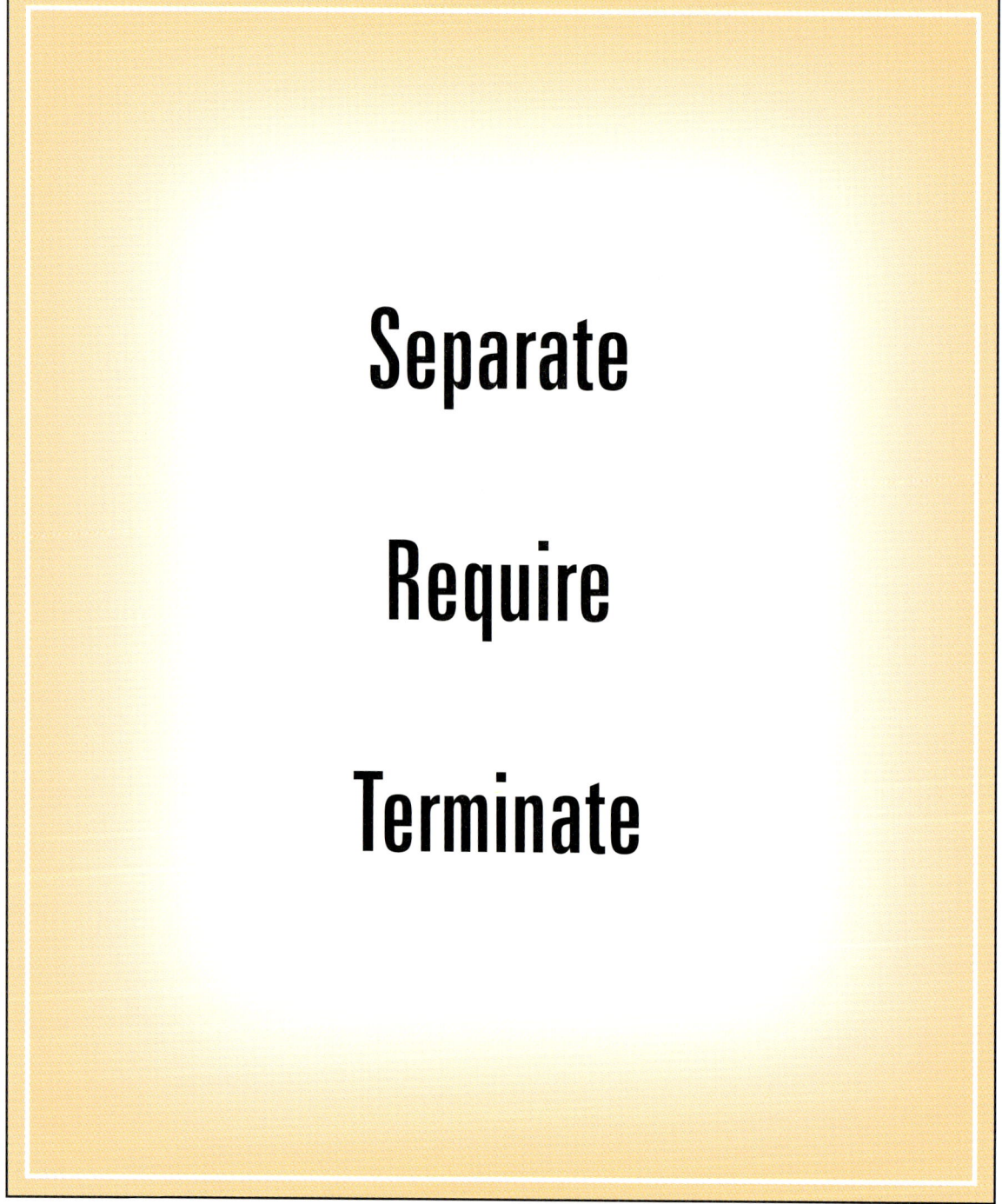

If one or more are unwilling to reconvene at a later date, or if the participants are too openly hostile to be reasonable in the opinion of the facilitator— If, for instance, one person is able to intimidate the other beyond a hope for open candid discussion,— there are three options.

1. **Separate the people so they do not have to relate to each other on a regular basis.** Note: one or all are likely to re-ignite similar conflicts in their new teams no matter where they are, so you may just be postponing the inevitable. Postponement is sometimes a good strategy in business, but only if a time line is set and an appropriate re-hiring, training or other strategy is implemented during the postponement— something which will make the decision clearer or make the cost of firing an employee less costly for the company.

2. **Terminate the employment of one or more of the participants in the conflict.** It is amazing what happens within a department or small company when a major source of conflict is removed. The people remaining feel honored by the act. They also know they will be held accountable for their ability to increase their professionalism and job performance. As a result the whole team benefits.

3. **Require that one or more of the participants in the conflict obtain professional counseling or job training help,** depending upon what the source of the conflict is determined to be. If this requirement is put forth, set a date for a meeting at which time the issues will be re-addressed and the conflict resolution process will be reconvened one last time.

10

Control, Caretaking and Other Terrible Habits

One of the factors which drove the development of the Professional Personality Index was a proliferation of personality tests which classify people as being controlling people, or caretakers (people pleasers), assigning these characteristics as primary traits.

While these modes of behavior seem to be more apparent in certain personality styles, I became aware through my own self-discovery that I and every person I know are involved in the battle for control, and at certain times and in a variety of ways, one of the means of control which each of us may choose is caretaking, or people pleasing.

The reason each of us has chosen to be the way we are is related, as discussed earlier, to our genetic pre-disposition and to the parenting we received (or did not receive). Some of us learned to do open battle and to move aggressively for control of situations. Others of us learned that such an approach led to failure because someone else had more power to begin with or was more skilled in battle.

For these persons, another more subtle, but equally effective means to gain control was found through taking care of the needs of others. This strategy builds a certain level of obligation on the part of those around the caretaker. It also builds a dependency and an illusion of control which creates a lessening of aggression from more overtly controlling people.

We are all involved in the struggle for control. Some of us use caretaking as a means to obtain more control. I have found in my work as a change agent in companies, that the caretakers cause just as many problems, if not more, than the overtly controlling people, whether they be Builders, Merchants, Innovators or Bankers.

Caretaking people tend to be passive aggressive personalities, unwilling to take an open stand but willing, like everyone else, to continue to pursue the things they want. This indirect strategy, especially since it comes toward the recipient in the guise of a wolf in sheep's clothing, is confusing, manipulative and difficult to read. People who work with caretaking people don't feel a lot of pressure to perform job tasks, but they do feel pressure to behave in certain ways, to speak in certain tones of voice and to fit in.

Also, since caretaking people do not create clean boundaries in interpersonal relationships or in job relationships, they create an environment of chaos and distrust, wherein no one dares to make a decision for fear of "disappointing" the caretaker. They do not set high standards or hold people accountable because that feels to them like overt control tactics and they have learned that, for them, these control tactics are not safe or effective. To do so would also create the true impression that the Caretaker is also wanting to control things. This truth would create a level of integrity the caretaker is unwilling to assume at this time.

The reason we don't set high standards or hold people accountable to high expectations is that we are terrified that we will be required to live up to these same standards. In fact, we **are** required by others to meet our own standards. That is the single best reason for setting high standards and holding others accountable for performance. We will risc to the requirements just as sincerely as those around us.

Other nasty habits which are practiced by all four personality styles are: Passive aggression, Poor Me victim complaints, depression, anxiety, anger and rage, withholding feelings, discounting of others, etc.

It is reasonable to make the generalization, however that certain behaviors seem to fit better with certain personality styles, the most notorious being, that controlling tactics are most often adopted as part of the arsenal of Builders and Bankers, while Merchants and Innovators tend to opt for the land mine approach of caretaking.

11

Development of Personnel as a Means to Corporate Success

If every business problem is a people problem as has been proposed, then the only effective path to business success is the development of people. This can be done in two ways.

    First, attract and hire good quality people. This sounds easy and sounds like an end in itself, but I have found that hiring one good person is a significant challenge. Hiring two good people who have the necessary skills and who work well together is another challenge all together, something like winning the lottery every time it occurs.

One of my clients continuously recites quotations from business gurus who recommend such things as:

    "If they can't do the job, find someone who can."

    "Turn your people over at least once a year. It's good for business."

The reality is, that managers who tend to function under these kinds of assumptions are themselves ineffective and should be turned-over and spanked.

This is not to say that clear business objectives do not need to be set and met and that some employees are simply not productive or are not good team members. Some are disruptive or choose to be blocks to necessary changes. We have discussed this previously.

But it is important to realize that we spend a significant amount of time and money building and nurturing good customer relations, good banking relations, good vendor relations. It seems appropriate to invest an equal if not greater energy and resource allocation toward the development of the individuals in our business organization. This, after all, is the way we increase our capacity to build all of the other necessary relations with the economic world outside our offices.

I have known numerous business leaders who have attempted to become better business people by getting more business education. And to some degree this has been helpful. But how many of us today realize that an MBA is an MBA, a piece of paper which affirms a certain level of classical knowledge in several subjects, but it does not certify power, wisdom, or love, innate capability, management and team building abilities or anything else directly related to running a successful business.

An MBA illustrates best that a person has the basic intelligence to learn from books and lectures.

When I want an employee to perform a certain task I am most concerned about whether he or she has the innate characteristics which are most suited toward the job I want to get done. My second concern is "To what degree has this been demonstrated by successful experiences?" I have hired many people who had the right experience and a good resume but when hired demonstrated to me that their capabilities were misaligned to the job. The sales person I hired really should have been an accountant. The manager I hired should never have been taken off the production line.

The only path I know toward consistent success in business is to find people who are "meant for the job" and who have the skills necessary to perform. From that base I can build any business. It is not possible to start with people whose personalities and capabilities are mismatched to the job (no matter what experiences appear on their resume) and teach them skills and end up with more than a barely acceptable situation. Generally we end up with a great deal of conflict, job malfunction, errors, team unrest and business failure.

So, smart business owners and managers will use a profiling test like the Professional Personality Index in order to understand the right person for the job position. This information added to an assessment of basic skills and experience increases dramatically the likelihood of hiring a good fit for the job.

12

Learning Styles

Each personality type learns by different means, so all training must be developed to accommodate the various personality styles in order to optimize effectiveness.

Builders, for instance learn by doing. They take action, observe their results and take another action, course correcting as they go. Their high degree of spontaneity is stifled and they become very frustrated in a rote learning or highly structured setting which prohibits their kind of free flow activity. Builders like to get up and move around, and hate being hemmed in. They like personal space. Builders can't hear you if you sit too close.

Merchants learn by talking. They talk through their ideas, course correcting as they go, always listening to their own words and evaluating the appropriateness of each conclusion. They drive other people crazy with their seeming inconsistency. Merchants really aren't that inconsistent. They are constantly in process and therefore almost everything they say is being modified as they speak.

PROFESSIONAL PERSONALITY INDEX™
Basis For Success

BUILDER
Energy
Compulsion
Strength

MERCHANT
Belief
Risk
Spontaneity

BANKER
Carefulness
Test/Prove
Safety

INNOVATOR
Tenacity
Reason
Thorough

© Copyright Lynn Ellsworth Taylor, November 1997

Merchants are like Innovators in the fact that they hate to finish a good idea, a good vision before they perfect it. To do the perfecting they keep talking. Brainstorming sessions with others, especially Innovators who add juice and complexity to the ideas of Merchants are a wonderful extension of the Merchant's learning process.

So, games, exercises, group projects, dramatic presentations. All of these learning approaches appeal to Merchants. Like Builders, Merchants also like to be highly active. Don't leave them sitting too long. Make time for them to talk.

Innovators learn by invention. Give Innovators partial sentences that they have to complete. Give them a problem to solve independently or corporately. Give them a game with clear objectives and lots of obstacles in the way. Give them a maze with five end points but only one with the cheese at the end. Innovators learn by ciphering, computing, assessing, evaluating, postulating.

Innovators are more visually oriented than Merchants and Builders. Visual resources provide additional stimulation to an Innovator's need to assess information as they pursue the right solution. Don't tell Innovators the answers, they'll just disagree. Ask them to find the answers themselves and they'll consider you a genius.

Bankers learn through analysis. They are highly visually oriented, like to sit and listen and take notes. They like to record hundreds of facts and figures, see proofs actualized, hear evidence that supports the visual data and then be given an opportunity to rearrange the data so it is more perfect.

Give Bankers the task of recording all learning information, of researching additional information which supports or refutes that which is presented and then presenting in visual form the results of their findings. Put it in writing.

Bankers learn by analyzing data, mostly from visual sources or formal presentation. Give Bankers games to play and too much free time and they'll freeze up and refuse to participate.

Believe it or not, Bankers are having fun when they are learning their way.
Believe it or not, Bankers, Merchants do learn as they play.

PROFESSIONAL PERSONALITY INDEX™: Basis For Success

BUILDER
Gut Level
Decisive
Powerful

MERCHANT
Inspired
Energized
Exciting

INTUITIVE

BANKER
Analytical
Formulative
Solid

INNOVATOR
Perceptive
Adaptive
Resourceful

COGNITIVE

© Copyright Lynn Ellsworth Taylor, November 1997

13

Building Effective Teams

There are three important avenues of information which need to be tracked in parallel as we attempt to build effective business teams.

First we must fully understand the purpose and the primary function of the team, its contribution to the overall company objectives. This analysis must be thorough enough that each activity required of the team can be broken into individual tasks with time estimates established.

Second we must understand the constraints of budget. Part of this avenue of analysis involves a comparison and prioritization of the subject team's relative importance when compared with other teams and its consumption of resources compared with its contribution to the whole. Given that rational conclusions have been drawn in this second process, we return to the first avenue of thought and re-prioritize the functions and tasks of the subject team in order to see which might be delayed, reduced in scope or eliminated.

Third, we must assess the existing team members, evaluating their effectiveness, efficiency and consistency in the performance of each essential task. When compared against a Professional

Personality Index of all the members, we will often discover that the first order of business is to shift tasks around among the existing members, or if we have a large company, to trade team members with other departments.

Since it takes a great deal more time and energy to perform tasks for which we are not qualified, or not predisposed to enjoy or perform well, this realignment very often eliminates the need to increase staff size. Often we find that we will accomplish far more by eliminating team members than we would by enlarging the group.

A good example of this reality occurred with a commodity products distributor. The company's sales had dropped off by 30% over the previous six months and the company president was stressed and under personal tax pressure. He was constantly trying to retrain new sales people. He was running back and forth between territories like a juggler with plates spinning on sticks. He had as many plates spinning in the air as his energy would allow and still he was failing.

The company's sales staff was making a sub-industry income and their turn-over rate was nearly 60% per quarter. This is not a formula for success.

The president and his sales manager who was also not in a territory were both Merchant/Builders as were the two best performing sales people. We cut the staff in half, doubling the size of each person's territory, keeping only Merchant/Builders.

Next we shifted our method of selling to the smaller customers from a route sales approach to an inventory stocking program with telephone sales stretching the need for site visits from once per week to once every six weeks. We applied the excess energy to pursuit of the next larger-sized accounts.

Within three months we were setting new sales records, doubling the business in just six months. The sales people were making more than 50% above industry averages. Turnover went to 0% over the next two years and the average order size doubled.

We now had the right people doing the right jobs and doing them the right way. When we hired our next sales person to support new product lines, we hired a Builder/Merchant who wanted to make better than the industry average and was willing to work our system to do it.

Another example is a telecommunications company which had a technical support group answering phones, a customer service group, a dispatch group controlling the technical staff resources, account managers who felt responsibility for customer satisfaction and obtaining add-on sales, field sales reps who would also receive calls from urgent customers and a management staff with equal commitments to customer satisfaction. Everyone felt over-worked. Everyone was receiving customer complaint calls. Everyone was making promises to fix.

The solution we were hired to install was the addition of appropriate new personnel who could finally make customers happy— make everyone more effective by reducing the work load.

The solution we installed was a 30% reduction in staff size, eliminating the customer service group which had no authority to dispatch or make financial accommodations, and eliminating the project management group which was also being used to clean up the messes caused by poor work orders and poor technician training. This reduction plus a few systems and procedures which defined who was able to do what and who was responsible for what when— caused an increase of company profit from a 3% loss to a nine percent pretax gain, with an increase of customer satisfaction beyond measure. We did this in less than 30 days, all based upon realignment of people according to the Professional Personality Index and the processes described in this Resource Guide.

14

Using the Professional Personality Index to Characterize

Job Positions, Company and Department Indexes

The Professional Personality Index can be effectively utilized to profile your company, your department or a specific position within any organization. The process is simple. Whether the process is performed by one or more persons, follow these simple steps.

1. Briefly answer the following questions regarding the subject job position, company or department:

    A. What is the primary purpose, primary function?

    B. Which one or two tasks are performed most often?

    C. Who does this person or group of people most often serve?

    D. What relationship(s) will most impact success?

    E. What mistake(s) are the easiest to make?

    F. Describe how success for this person, company or department looks and feels.

G. Describe in detail a person you know who is filling a similar position effectively (or a company or department which is effective in the same business). What are the critical elements which are present in these known situations?

2. Having answered these questions take a Professional Personality Index test as though you were the company, department or job position in question. In other words circle those words in each box which best describe the person required for the open position, or which best describe the character traits most needed in the company or department.

Asking several people to participate in this process can be highly informative. Once each person has filled out the test, total all results together and study your results. You should come up with a result which appears something like this: Builder— 72, Merchant— 18, Innovator— 54, Banker— 36.

If you are interested in more information, simply study the scores of individual words, i.e.: Action 32, Teach 3, etc. This simple study will reveal a wealth of information regarding the optimum balance for the position, company or department. By giving the Professional Personality Index test to all people involved with or being considered for positions in question, you are more likely to select appropriate individuals. You may also find it quite simple to re-engineer your company or department by applying the results of all the tests administered.

Taking this kind of approach gives any business and its management an incredible advantage over others who attempt the same process using only personal experience, interviewing skills and long term performance evaluations.

In my business management practice I am often able to effect a re-engineering of a company or department within the first few hours of involvement. And, very important, is the fact that all people effected are also involved in and informed regarding the process. I find that I have to do very little work, other than administer the tests, facilitate the communications regarding test results and lead a group process to enhance group performance.

15

Even Companies Have an Optimum Personality Index

As we have discussed briefly in Chapters 13. and 14., companies and departments within companies also have their own unique personality style. Companies in early development will be built around the personality of the business owner. In the early stages this is highly appropriate since business owners tend to select business areas for which they have an affinity and their personality styles are usually suited for their work. Since most of us naturally choose people we like the growing company continues to be balanced around the personality of the owner.

As the company succeeds, however, the demands for administration, customer service, production and production management, quality control, accounting and finance, etc. begin to demand greater and greater energy. The personality of the company must evolve with these demands inviting into the spectrum of employees people who do not necessarily fit comfortably with the original personality style of the founder.

This evolution is always disruptive and sometimes painful. Wrong choices are often made, requiring growth of staff through a process of trial and error and error and error. Application of the Professional Personality Index in these instances can greatly reduce the ineffectiveness of such a growth process.

Another common situation is a department or company which has been in existence for some time without change of personnel, often without any re-alignment of people and jobs. The reality is that the world and its markets continue to change. If a company or department has been static in its application of people resources for more than two years, you can bet the efficiency and appropriateness of job assignments is significantly misaligned.

Again, by evaluating the optimum personality style which is now required by a company or department and comparing that optimum profile with actual tests of all players, we can rapidly determine who, where and in which positions changes are required. Often a simple shuffle of job assignments, an exchange of tasks among the players can create a tremendous increase of energy and improve results. Sometimes there is a need to bring in new energy or eliminate people who are committed to resisting required change. The Professional Personality Index makes these sometimes painful decisions more clear and less personal.

16

Employment Decisions

Those who wish to use the Professional Personality Index for job screening or to create more clarity around a termination decision are encouraged to do so. This test is designed to provide immediate informative results within ten minutes. These results have a high degree of accuracy in classifying persons according to personal values, personality traits and characteristics. Many individual business values and beliefs are also revealed through this test.

Please be cautioned, however, that a purely statistical, or "black and white" application of the test results is not recommended. The test is meant to provide additional, valuable information over and above that which can be gained through interviewing or skills testing. People, however, constantly defy tests such as these and we who want to be most effective will never put aside wholly our own gut level instincts, nor should we.

Bob Tace, a nationally recognized consultant recommends a 30% weighting of the Professional Personality Index, combined with "fire in the eye" at 20%, skills testing at 20%, gut feeling at 20% and resume and experience at 10%.

One field salesman comes to mind who proves the point. Jim is a sales representative for a Chemical and Supply Distributor. He is a strong Builder/Banker. My choice of the optimum personality for his position would be a Builder/Innovator with substantial Merchant characteristics, or a Merchant/Innovator with sufficient Builder characteristics to provide closing and pursuit energy.

The Innovator was an important element in this job position, since each customer quotation required assessment of a customer's needs for technical equipment, determination of production levels, optimum facilities usage and many other complex factors which only an Innovator could develop effectively.

Had I taken the results of the Professional Personality Index solely and literally, I would have been forced to replace Jim. Instead, we shifted our focus to an assessment of the entire sales staff, including customer service people who manned the phones. By taking the whole group into consideration, we found that Jim was the only Builder and the only Banker personality in the entire group.

Firing Jim would have been a major error. There were already more than enough Innovators to solve technical problems and more than enough Merchants to build and maintain good relationships with customers. Jim's Builder/Banker personality brought balance to the company. The task remained to be certain we designed our sales and marketing process to fully accommodate a Builder/Banker in the field.

Please be careful and considered in your application of these test results. This being said, you will find that most of the time the test results provide a clear picture of a person's attributes and values and, to the degree you have determined what kind of person will best fit a job position, your staffing decisions will be more successful if you find a good match validated by the Professional Personality Index.

17

Taking and Giving the Test

The Professional Personality Index test is very simple. The instructions are clearly expressed on the printed individual test sheets. The essentials are as follow:

1. It is best to take the test without knowing even the names of the Basic Personality Styles. So don't read or allow your participants to read about the Index prior to the test.

2. The test should take about seven to ten minutes including the time its takes to count each circled word in each category. Stress taking less than ten seconds to mark the words in each box. 36 boxes X 10 seconds = 360 seconds = 6 minutes. This leaves plenty of time to count all of the A, B, C, and D. words circled.

3. Each participant must circle two words, and only two words in each box.

4. After completing the test each participant is asked to tear off the Index Key card at the vertical perforation. The words in each box are scrambled so it is important to use the Key card. Align the numbered letter boxes on the key card with the numbered word boxes on the test and count the A, B, C, and D words,

moving the key card to the right across the rows, being careful to align the correct key to the corresponding word box as shown below. Note the rows are marked 1-9 as are the key boxes with the jumbled letters A, B, C, and D.

5. Enter the total of all A, B, C, and D words in the total spaces at the bottom of the test sheet.

6. Mark the Professional Personality Index on the lower half of the key card with the total of each Index. Mark the Index along the diagonal in each quadrant.

7. Connect the dots. Some individuals may wish to color in the indexes by quadrant in order to more clearly illustrate their Professional Personality Index.

8. Turn the test sheet over to find the names of your dominant (highest score, A., B., C., or D.) and Secondary (next highest score) indexes. Fill in the blanks below your Professional Personality Index chart with your Dominant and Secondary names.

   A. Builder,   B. Merchant,

   D. Banker,   C. Innovator.

9. Read the brief description regarding all four Personality styles. In many instances this brief description will be sufficient to start discussions or to continue a job interview.

Completing a Testing Session

Having taken this test yourself, encourage others in your team to take the same test. Share your results with each other. The chosen facilitator might provide an overview of the detailed discussion of each personality found in this Resource Guide in Chapters 2, 3, and 4.

After each of you have reported your own findings about yourself, ask for feedback on the appropriateness and completeness of each person's self assessment. Ask specifically for information concerning areas where personal strategies are ineffective in the job assigned, especially in relationship with specific team members.

When these areas are uncovered, be careful not to defend yourself or each other. Set some ground rules beforehand, requiring each person who wishes to engage another, to first ask permission to give feedback. Otherwise encourage attentive listening and non-aggressive questioning.

The prime motive of all involved is to learn what approach might be more effective with the person being questioned and with the person giving feedback. You are not always right, you know. Maybe you don't know. Ask your team.

Feedback is only feedback. Encourage everyone to take it, think about it, use what feels most important and appropriate.

Be kind to each other. Be forgiving of yourself.

It is important to give each participant the opportunity to agree or disagree with the Index which is developed from their test. Allow open discussion of any specific descriptions of strengths or weaknesses of the various Personality styles.

This allows each person to "own" the balance of the expressed characteristics to which they have no objection.

If the test is being used for quick assessment for hiring and job change situations, this open discussion and a comparison of the Professional Personality Index with the person's job or proposed job will be educational for both the participant and the test facilitator.

If the purpose of the test is to develop a Personality profile of a department or an entire company, more thorough discussions, learning sessions, seminars and team re-organization sessions are strongly advised.

Warning— No one person should give this test to a group of people and make arbitrary judgments and decisions from these test results alone. No person or test is that perceptive when it comes to understanding companies, the demands of individual job positions or the capacities of individuals. This Professional Personality Index is designed to facilitate dialogue, open communications, develop understanding and consensus and cause strategic thinking for all parties involved. If used with respect and care it is a powerful tool. If used to control and manipulate or to make black and white decisions, it can be a destructive tool. Don't abuse this educational resource.

18

No More Excuses

Now that you have a precise and easy to use Professional Personality Index, there is no reason not to put it to use in every situation possible. It is no longer necessary to remain ignorant regarding the personality styles of yourself and the people who work with you or for other parts of your company.

The knowledge provided by the Professional Personality Index is fundamental to all job assignments, hiring and firing, training procedures, reorganizations and most other internal company decisions involving people.

Business managers have to manage every resource within their grasp in order to survive, in order to grow and build strong businesses. We tend to be adequate cash managers, inventory builders, customer and market managers, production managers. But when it comes to people management we often throw up our hands in disbelief and frustration, or give the ill-considered command, "If you can't get it done, I'll hire someone who can!"

Trouble in business begins with the hiring process, which is based on published resumes listing a person's own perception of job skills, desired opportunity and work history. The hiring process seldom reveals a potential employee's personality traits, innate leadership strategies, or their style of thinking.

We have often heard of left-brained and right-brained people, but nothing provides us with an easy quantification of these mental approaches. Even if a tool offered easy access to this information, we would still be pressed to develop our own understanding of how to apply this knowledge to specific job requirements.

The fact is that there are many such assessment tools available today. In the next century few persons will be hired without undergoing a personality and leadership style assessment. The reason— performance on the job is far more determined by basic personality styles and communications styles than skills developed through work experiences. In the 21st Century the average person will change careers 3-5 times.

The trouble continues after a person is hired. Personnel are assigned to departments to work under managers who may or may not approach life in a similar manner. Often variances in personality style result in conflict, passive aggressive behavior, open hostility, subterfuge. The problems are more often linked to simple differences in style than to job related substance, and yet they consume valuable business energy— these conflicts waste human resources.

The typical response to such people issues is to begin treating the employees or managers as children, telling them what to do, reprimanding all concerned for their ineffectiveness, reinforcing fully understood business goals and objectives— all of which only deepens the conflict, frustrates the team, and consumes more energy.

What is not done, is a full scale assessment of each individual, comparing the individual's personal strategies to the job being demanded of them. Open sessions in which all players are able to hear the various characteristics, strengths and weaknesses of other personality styles, increase communications, decrease hostilities and open the doors to tangible changes— a realignment of human resources toward more optimum utility.

It has been my experience that people, once made aware of their personality style, and that of those around them, rapidly respond by joining together to face problems, generate creative solutions, and build a team effort. This awareness itself, even without protracted training, offers most people enough knowledge that they as a group can make significant strides toward focusing their energies on business tasks, rather than non-productive positioning of one person against the other.

What business managers do not know about their employees controls the company. What the employees and owners don't know about themselves and each other, how they function and think, how they approach life— this ignorance dictates business results more than any other factor. And yet our understanding and knowledge of our most important resource is usually the last thing we consider when trying to solve a business problem.

There is no business problem which is not, in fact, a people problem. There is no business solution which is not, in fact, a people based solution. Business managers must learn that people resources cannot be managed from a position of ignorance any more than can the accounting functions of the company. We must strengthen our knowledge in this area dramatically in the U.S. in order to maintain our competitive edge in the next decade and beyond.

We are past the time when hard nosed business owners can push this kind of thinking off as "touchy feelie stuff," or "baby-sitting." The reality is that the business leaders who find themselves making this kind of derogatory statement are those who are most ignorant of the power of appropriate human resource management; the pure effects which can be measured on the bottom line.

Just as there is no license required for procreating and raising children, there is no knowledge required for hiring and managing people. Just being a company owner, or a department manager suddenly makes me an expert. Most of us experts fail occasionally in this area, at least with certain types of personalities. We are either constantly hiring people who irritate and frustrate us, or gather people around us who we like but can't seem to get the job done.

Before you make your next hire or job termination, learn more about yourself and your personality style, your strategies for getting what you want. Learn more about the personality style that will best fit your job opening, and then measure each potential candidate before making your decision.

You don't buy a computer without considering its appropriateness for the tasks required. Why hire a person without assessing the appropriateness of the personality for the tasks required.

It's not possible to separate a person from his or her personality and changes in people are slow to come. Hire the person you want and need the first time and save money, time and emotional stress. In order to manage your human resources, you must know your human resources. Success in business depends on it.

About the Author

Lynn Ellsworth Taylor

Lynn was born in Seattle, Washington in 1949. Graduated from Warner Pacific College, Portland, Oregon, in 1971 with a degree in literature. He studied briefly under William Stafford while in Portland. Completed post graduate work at the University of Washington, 1972. Lynn has worked as a window cleaner, teacher, poet, marketing executive, sales VP and CEO of a publicly traded high technology speech recognition company. He is currently serving as president of Elliott Bay Management Group, Inc., a business management company in Seattle.

Elliott Bay Management has served more than 400 business owners in their quest to create valuable stable companies. Lynn and his partner, Jerry Marble, provide business assessments followed by performance based management contracts. They constantly improve cash flow, generate higher gross margins, increase sales and create substantially greater profits for their client owners. The Professional Personality Profile was created by Lynn to enhance his ability to relate effectively with business owners and to help business owners balance their management and support teams for greater effectiveness.

Lynn's love for presentations of poems and teaching has tuned his ear, sharpened his wit and deepened his appreciation of poetry as communication. Taylor has taught poetry at Boise State College (Adult Education), University of Washington Experimental College, Telshi Yeshiva Rabbinical School (Cleveland, Ohio) and at several high schools in Washington State. Lynn continues to work as a businessman-poet. He is currently preparing his fourth collection of poems for publication.

Lynn has performed his poetry monthly at Barnes & Noble book stores over the past two years. He is the director of the CPC Community Ensemble. He composes music, sings and plays the piano. He is the father of two teenage boys. Lynn and his wife and sons live in Federal Way, Washington south of Seattle.

ABOUT THE AUTHOR

Publishing Credits
Literary Lion 1966, 1967.
Pylon 1967, 1968, 1969, 1970.
Reach Magazine 1971, 1972.
Editor, Junior Writers' Magazine 1971-1973. circ. 50,000.
Gold Quill, Inc., Nampa, Idaho, **Poetic Moods**, a collection of poems. 1972.
Maxwell-Lee Publishing Company, Cleveland, Ohio. **Don't Bury the Child**, a collection of poems. 1976.
Euclid News Journal, 1978.
Class Magazine, November 1993.
Gaia Publishing Company, Seattle, WA, **Flying Home**, a collection of poems, 1990.
Federal Way City Herald, 1992.
Jeopardy, Spring, 1990.
First Time, Editions 24 and 25.
Poetalk, 1992, 1993, 1994.
Art Times, 1994.

Readings
Boise State College, 1972.
Idaho State Teachers Association, 1972.
Idaho PTA, annual assembly, 1973.
WELW Radio, 1976.
Gildenmeister's, Euclid, Ohio., 1977.
Channel 5, Cleveland, Ohio, 1977.
Bread and Circuses Theater, Poet in Residence, 1973-1977. Weekly readings.
University of Washington, 1978.
University Presbyterian Church, 1979.
Blue Moon Cafe, 1979.
Red Dust Poetry Theater, 1982.
Westminster Presbyterian Church, 1991.
Elliott Bay Book Company, April, 1992.
Washington Strawberry Festival, 1993.
Washington State Chapter of the National Writer's Association, 1993.
Washington Poet's Association, Annual Meeting, 1992.
King County Libraries- Multiple branch library readings, 1992 - 1993.
Warner Pacific College, 1994.
Community Presbyterian Church, 1992,1994.
Burien Arts Commission, 1995
Barnes & Noble Bookstore, April, 1996 to present

Special Recognition
Washington State Poet's Association, **Charlie Award**, First Place Humorous poem.
Poet in Residence, Bread and Circuses Theater, Shaker Heights, Ohio, 1974 - 1976.

Elliott Bay Publishing Company proudly offers, for Individuals, Companies, Churches and Organizations

Effective Leadership Training Seminars

Based on the life changing book — How Can They Possibly Think Like That???
By Lynn Ellsworth Taylor

Participants in this class will learn more about themselves and their relationships with others in less time and with a more concrete and usable framework than any other leadership training available.

- Take the Professional Personality Index (PPI) test
- Learn to be more effective with difficult people.
- Learn what makes you difficult to deal with.
- Learn how to lead with your most powerful personality traits.

These seminars offer a balance of learning opportunities, lecture, games, small group interactions, personal exercises. They may be customized for various business and group requirements and are facilitated by the author or by senior executive consultants personally trained by the author. Participants learn the power of self-knowledge combined with communications and leadership skills.

Spiritual cornerstones cause value sets to be adopted

Values cause judgments to be made

Judgments (choices) determine behavior

Behavior creates predictable results.

For Information and Prices Call 206-283-8144

Check out our web site at www.nvst.com/personality

What you don't know about yourself costs you and your company every day.